with CHRIST *at the* THRONE *of* GOD

Volume One

ROBERT MAASBACH

Grosvenor House
Publishing Limited

This book is published by
Grosvenor House Publishing Ltd
28-30 High Street, Guildford, Surrey, GU1 3EL.
www.grosvenorhousepublishing.co.uk

A CIP record for this book
is available from the British Library

ISBN 978-1-78148-828-7

Abbreviations

The following versions of the Bible have been used in this book:

NKJV (New King James Version)
TEV (Today's English Version)
AMPB (Amplified Bible)
LB (Living Bible)
NLT (New Living Translation)

Generally, unless otherwise indicated, scriptures quoted are from the NKVJ.

Please note that on many occasions Bible verses and phrases have been paraphrased and are not intended as an exact rendering of recognised translations. References have then been given to aid the reader in their personal study and understanding of what is being shared.

Introduction

Over many years, the Holy Spirit kept making me aware that the Lord Jesus desired me to write this devotional book and some other books besides. Then in September of 2009, God spoke His word to me not to delay but obey.

As we walk with Jesus through this life, we learn from Him that when God speaks by His Spirit it is always *now* He wants us to obey. The perfect time to do anything is when God speaks, for those who obey will see His Spirit enable them to do what He says.

For the last three and half years, I have sat before the Lord writing this first volume, and while there were many days it seemed as if I was digging through my earthly feelings, the Holy Spirit helped me to find the true gold and share some of its riches in these pages. The gold I am referring to is the main theme of this book – namely, 'The Life that Jesus has with the Father.'

In the first volume, my prayer is that you will find the grace of Jesus drawing you up into the Life He has with the Father, so that you may know inwardly that Jesus is in the Father and that as He lives you may live also.

Oh, how the Lord Jesus longs for you to live in the freedom He gives, as He Himself took all our sins and infirmities in His body on the cross to free us forever from their awful grip. Once Jesus had done all that was needful for the cleansing of your sins in His own blood and the clearing of your record of every charge, He ascended to the throne of God to give you the Holy Spirit who proceeds from the Father, so you may live as He lives, in perfect righteousness, peace and joy.

Dear child of God, the riches of the glory of the Life Jesus has with the Father are immeasurably great. Because of the love Jesus has demonstrated in all He has done for you, it is His joy in doing the will of the Father, to assure your heart before Him in faith, that out of the fullness of His Life with the Father He will give you grace upon grace, blessing upon blessing and gifts heaped upon gifts (John 1:16).

Let me say this again, that it is the joy of the Lord Jesus, as well as a mark of His great love for you, to give you continuously and forever the richest measure of the divine presence of the Father, so that you may come to the fullness of His stature and like Him become a body wholly filled and flooded with the Life of God Himself.

I pray that as you are reading this devotional, that the Holy Spirit will open your eyes to see that Jesus has all the power and authority to accomplish this in you, exceedingly abundantly above all that you would know how to ask for or could ever think of, for this is the loving purpose of the Father for you in Christ Jesus.

Now to God be glory in the church by Christ Jesus to all generations, forever and ever. Amen (Ephesians 3:21).

A little while longer and the world will see Me no more, but you will see Me. Because I live, you will live also

John 14:19

In these seven words, 'Because I live, you will live also' - spoken by Jesus the night before He died - the disciples were given a revelation of God's plan for man. In Jesus they saw the glory of the Life He has with the Father, a Life full of grace and truth. They loved being with Jesus for being with Him was the same as being with God. Everything came alive in His presence; His words were like the breath of God, full of the Holy Spirit, like everlasting light flooding their hearts and minds. And, oh the wonders of His compassion with which they saw Him love and heal people. They had given up everything to be with Jesus. They could not imagine living without Him. He was their life.

Now Jesus showed them that as He lived they would live also. The same heavenly Life that emanated from His person would be in them.

Dear child of God, this is why Jesus is now at the throne of God, so that He can empower and uphold you with the Life He has with the Father.

This is the central theme and message of my book, 'With Christ at the Throne of God'. It is all about the wonder of His Life unfolding in you. My prayer as you open the pages of this devotion is that the Holy Spirit will flood your being with the riches of the glory of the Life Jesus has with the Father until you become a body wholly filled and flooded with God Himself.

This Life with the Father you see in Jesus is far more glorious than you can imagine; it is above all that you would dare ask or think, infinitely beyond your highest prayers, desires, hopes or dreams.

This Life Jesus has with the Father is now living in you, so that as He is with the Father so are you in the world (1 John 4:17).

This is the love of the Father for you, this is Christianity; the Life Jesus has with the Father in you!

Let's pray: Heavenly Father, in Your presence there is fullness of joy and at Your right hand are pleasures forevermore. Thank You for loving me and giving me the Life Jesus has with You in heaven so that as He lives I may live also.

In Jesus' name, Amen!

As the living Father sent Me, and I live because of the Father, so he who feeds on Me will live because of Me

John 6:57

Jesus called God the 'Living Father'. The wonderful Life you see in Jesus was the Life given to Him by the Living Father. Jesus came forth from God and was indwelled and upheld by Him. Jesus knew the Life He lived came from above and flowed through Him like a river. That is why He said, 'I have come to give you Life and more abundantly' (John 10:10).

Now let the Life you see in Jesus fill your heart. Just as the sun uninterruptedly shines forth its light and warmth, so the ascended Jesus gives you His Life from the throne of God. Truly you have everything when you have Jesus, for it is through your union with Him that you are filled with God Himself (Colossians 2:9).

Therefore, let the tender roots of your faith grow deep into Jesus. Trust Him to nourish you with His Life. Become dependent on Him just as a child in the womb is dependent, to be kept and fed by the life of the mother. As it is written, 'in Him you live and move and have your being' (Acts 17:28).

This is the wonder of Christianity - that because He lives you will live also!

Jesus said, 'Behold, I stand at the door and knock. If anyone hears my voice and opens the door, I will come into him and dine with him, and he with Me' (Revelation 3:20).

Are you hungry? Then invite Jesus to come into your heart and nourish you with His life-giving presence.

Do you feel self-conscious? Are you reproached by evil? Then don't despair; you are just hungry and need to be fed with the Life Jesus has with the Father.

Be encouraged; the Holy Spirit is here to feed you with His Life so you will no longer feel sinful or self-conscious but Christ-conscious.

What joy and comfort it is to know that we are redeemed in order to enjoy the Life Jesus has with the Father.

Come to His table and feast on His Life today.

Let's pray: Heavenly Father, I thank You for feeding me with the Life Jesus has with You in heaven so that I may see You glorified in me. I choose to come to the banqueting table today to be nourished by Your life.

In Jesus' name, Amen!

Jesus said to him, 'Have I been with you so long and yet you have not known Me, Philip? He who has seen Me has seen the Father; so how can you say, 'Show us the Father'?'

John 14:9

Jesus is the brightness of God's glory and the express image of His person (Hebrews 1:3). He is God revealed in Man.

All through history, man sought to find the only true living God, the creator of heaven and earth, and while the glory of God is revealed in all that He has made, the masterpiece of His creation is man - both male and female, created in His image (Genesis 1:26).

Jesus came to show you what man created in God's image looks like, for it pleased God to dwell in Him and thereby to reveal the wonder of Christianity which is Christ in you (Colossians 1:27).

Jesus said, 'If God's word lives in you, you will recognise I came from Him. And if His love is in you, you will receive Me so that the Life you see in Me may be in you also' (John 5:38-40).

Jesus was completely free from sin for He was perfectly God-conscious. There was nothing in Jesus that made Him feel separated from God. This is why when you know Jesus you know God and when you see Him you see the Father.

While this represents the basics of Christianity it never loses its marvel. It is truly wonderful that he who receives Jesus the Son of God receives the Life He has with the Father (1 John 5:12). The Life Jesus lived as a man on earth is the Life of God and that Life He now gives to live in you.

I am so grateful that Jesus is equally available to all who call upon His name!

Never forget then that when you have Jesus you have all of God. For through your union with Him you are made perfectly one with the Father. When you rely on your own ability to stay one with God you will always struggle and suffer the pain of failure. But when you trust in Jesus, who is seated at His right hand, you will experience the Life and love He has with the Father, which is far more wonderful than the human mind can comprehend.

Come, dear child of God, place all your trust in Jesus. He will uphold you and perfect you in your oneness with the Father.

Look to Jesus and you will see the face of God!

Let's pray: Heavenly Father, I am so grateful to know You through Jesus Christ my Lord. I know I am now one with You and that nothing can separate me from Your love. I love You Heavenly Father.

In Jesus' name, Amen!

That they all may be one, as You Father, are in Me. And I in You; that they also may be one in us, that the world may believe that You sent Me.

John 17:21

The Life Jesus gives is a Life of perfect oneness with the Father. It is nothing less than what you see in Him.

Consider the greatness of your salvation by looking to Jesus, who is the author and finisher of your faith, for the Life He has with the Father is what He now gives to you.

He not only begins His Life in you at your conversion but maintains His Life in you through His heavenly ministry at the throne of God. Jesus Himself is the strength of your salvation; He is the Truth that you are loved by the Father and that you have eternal Life.

Jesus knows what it means to be loved by the Father for He said, 'The Father bears witness of Me and I know the witness He witnesses of Me is true' (John 5:32).

This is the true spirit of Christianity, that the Father Himself in His great love bears witness with your spirit that you are His child (Romans 8:16).

It is the witness of the Father that assures you that you are His child and strengthens your faith to overcome in this world, no matter how human you are.

Think about it, when Jesus was baptized, He prayed, heaven opened, the Holy Spirit came upon Him and God said, 'You are My beloved Son; in You I am well pleased' (Luke 3:21-22).

This oneness with the Father you see in Jesus is what He now gives to you!

It is the greatest gift you could ever receive and is continually given with immeasurable grace and truth.

Think about what great love the Father has bestowed on you that you should be called a child of God (1 John 3:1).

Let's pray: Heavenly Father, I love being one with You - just like Jesus - through Your Life in me. I believe You love me and I know I am Your child.

In Jesus' name, Amen!

And the glory which You have given Me I have given them, that they may be one just as we are one

John 17:22

May the glory of God fill your soul as you pray, 'Father, I thank You that the same glory You gave Jesus You have given me, the glory of being one with You.'

Oh dear child of God, there is no greater glory than to be one with the Father!

Never forget, you are raised with Jesus, you are made alive together with Him and His Life in you has made it possible for you to live in the love of the Father (Ephesians 2:1-10).

There's no need for you to sit in darkness anymore because through the Holy Spirit's work in your heart and mind you are continually being cleansed with the blood of Jesus so you can live free from the consciousness of sin.

Never again will you need to feel the awful pain of separation!

Being one with the Father means knowing that God is in you and you are in Him.

This is the normal Christian Life!

No more separation from the bright presence of the Father, but always enjoying the sunshine of His favour, having His thoughts guarding your heart and mind and keeping you in His perfect peace.

This is the work of His grace, the glory of His Life in you; it is endless and it will far surpass all your highest hopes and dreams.

You cannot imagine the glory of His Life in you with your own mind, but the Holy Spirit is here to reveal it in you. It is a Life of perfect oneness with the Father and the Son, it is wonderful, it is heavenly, it is holy, it is sinless, it knows no condemnation or separation, it is the Life Jesus has with the Father in you.

This is Christianity!

Let's pray: Heavenly Father, You have given me the glory of the Life Jesus has with You in heaven, the glory of being one with You. Truly Your loving-kindness is better than life. My lips shall praise You and I will forever bless You.

In Jesus' name, Amen!

I have been crucified with Christ; it is no longer I who live, but Christ in me; and the life which I now live in the flesh I live by faith in the Son of God, who loved me and gave Himself for me
Galatians 2:20

This Scripture opens wide the riches of Christ Jesus' love for you because it shows that He Himself has accomplished everything for you to live as He lives with the Father.

In His death on the cross Jesus freed you forever from your slavery to the sin nature, for God who is rich in mercy made you alive together with Jesus even though you were dead in sin. The Life you now live is therefore not your own; it is the Life of the Son of God who loves you and gave Himself for you.

While this is a living reality for me today, it only started to become clear to me when in 1978 I broke my neck in two places.

While in a coma Jesus appeared to me and asked, 'What have you done for Me in your life?'

While I could not answer Him He lovingly looked at me without condemnation.

When I awoke my father came to see me and said, 'Don't you think it is the grace of God you are not dead?'

With gratitude I wept as I gave my life to Jesus. Then His Life came into me and I was born again!

My father said, 'Son, you know your life is not your own; let's pray and go home,' and I was healed immediately!

This is the gift of the Son of God who loves me and gave Himself for me, that the Life He has with the Father He now lives in me.

Oh, the glory that floods my soul the more I think of His love for me. His love drives out all fear of what will happen when I see Him. This is why I am looking forward to seeing Jesus, who for the glory of His accomplished work will present us all to the Father radiant with His Life (Jude 24; Colossians 1:21-22).

It is for this reason that I love the first line of that old hymn, 'Blessed assurance Jesus is mine; oh, what a foretaste of glory divine'.

Let's pray: Heavenly Father, I know You love me, for the Life I now live is not my own; it is the Life Jesus has with You in heaven. I am so happy! I love You Father!

In Jesus' name, Amen!

Blessed assurance, Jesus is mine!
Oh, what a foretaste of glory divine!
Heir of salvation, purchase of God,
Born of His Spirit, washed in His blood.

Refrain:
This is my story, this is my song,
Praising my Saviour all
the day long; This is my story, this is my song,
Praising my Saviour all the day long.

Perfect submission, perfect delight,
Visions of rapture now burst on my sight;
Angels, descending, bring from above
Echoes of mercy, whispers of love.

Perfect submission, all is at rest,
I in my Saviour am happy and blest,
Watching and waiting, looking above,
Filled with His goodness, lost in His love.

Frances Crosby, 1873.

And God raised us up together, and made us sit together in the heavenly places in Christ Jesus

Ephesians 2:6

This is one of the greatest statements in the Bible concerning our true inheritance in Christ Jesus - that through His life in you, you are made alive with Him and are seated with Him in heaven. This is more real than you may know!

Please realise, precious child of God, your Heavenly Father has given all authority in heaven and earth to Jesus. He now reigns supreme because He overcame sin, Satan, and death. Yes, all enemies are under His feet so that the Life He now lives at the throne of God He can give to you.

Can you see why God calls you more than a conqueror? Because He provides for all your needs according to His riches in glory by Christ Jesus. Oh how the Holy Spirit yearns to reveal in you the Life and love Jesus has with the Father.

However earthly you may feel, your inheritance is to reign in life with Christ, and to do that right now through His Life in you.

The Apostles of old were people just like you and me. They believed in Jesus, the Son of God. When Peter and John were about to go into the temple in Jerusalem to pray, they spoke to a lame man who was wonderfully healed in Jesus' name. Peter said, 'Don't look at us as if through our own power or godliness we made this man walk. God glorified His servant Jesus, the Prince of Life whom He raised from the dead, and we are witnesses of this. It is through faith in His name that God has made this man strong, whom you see and know. Yes, the faith which comes through Him has given him this perfect soundness' (Acts 3:12-16).

You see the Life Jesus has at the throne of God had begun to flow through these two ordinary men through faith!

And the faith I am talking about is the faith Jesus our God and Saviour gives. This faith is a gift and this faith is in you who believe in Him. Now simply trust in Jesus and you will receive this wonderful Life He has with the Father. Jesus will reveal in you the Life you have seated with Him in heaven.

Let's pray: Heavenly Father, thank You for giving me faith in Jesus. I believe the Life You gave Jesus at Your right hand is in me. I trust You to show forth Your power and grace in me.

In Jesus' name, Amen!

But we have this treasure in earthen vessels that the excellence of the power may be of God and not of us

2 Corinthians 4:7

While the power and glory that fills your life through faith in Jesus is really from heaven, you are still human. You are still like an 'earthen vessel'.

What you need to remember when you feel so very earthly is that God is looking for yielded vessels, those in whom He can show Himself strong for the good of all men.

Today the world needs to see what God can do through someone wholly given to Him; for there is really nothing too difficult for the Lord if He has the right person to do it with.

The Apostle Paul was such a person who yielded himself to Jesus.

What amazing heavenly blessings Jesus was able to give to the whole world through him!

Paul said, 'This is a faithful saying and worthy of all acceptance, that Christ Jesus came into the world to save sinners of whom I am chief. However, for this reason I obtained mercy, that in me first Jesus might show all longsuffering, as a pattern to those who are going to believe on Him for everlasting life' (1Timothy 1:14-16).

In other words, Jesus can do anything in and through you if you fully yield yourself to Him.

Dear child of God, consider the first miracle Jesus worked at a wedding. The guests had run out of wine. Jesus asked them to take vessels used for water and fill them. As they filled them the miracle took place; the water was turned into the finest wine.

Now if the Lord Jesus can do this with water, how much more can He do it for you as you present yourself a willing vessel.

Always know it is the Father's great pleasure to fill you with the greatest measure of His Divine presence, so that like Jesus you may go about doing good and kind things for others which show you are His child.

It brings Him such joy to fill willing vessels like you with the glory of His Life!

Let's pray: Heavenly Father, here I am a willing vessel. I yield myself completely and thank You for filling me with the Holy Spirit, so that I can go about doing good and kind things for others which show I am Your child.

In Jesus' name, Amen!

But when it pleased God, who separated me from my mother's womb and called me through His grace, to reveal His Son in me, that I might preach Him

Galatians 1:15-16

Have you ever thought what God has called you to in life? Did you know that by His amazing grace He has called you into fellowship with His Son so that Jesus Himself may be revealed in you (1 Corinthians 1:9)?

The intimacy between you and Jesus is even more vital than the beating of your own heart.

This is the indescribable gift of God; the Life Jesus has with the Father in you.

This is why it is so important that Jesus is at the throne of God, so that He can empower you with His Life to live like Him (1 Peter 1:14).

You see when God made man He saw something most beautiful; He saw the son of man being the son of God. All through the scriptures you can see God work His plan for man which now is fulfilled in Jesus. Jesus the Son of Man is the Son of God.

Now God, who called you by His grace, has done this so that you can live like Jesus, as His child in the light of His presence on earth.

Living in the light of God's presence on earth is only possible because Jesus is at the throne of God, empowering you with the Life He has with the Father. And the reason there is so much power for you to live in God's presence is because the blood of Jesus keeps you cleansed.

You see according to His mercy God saved you, through the washing of regeneration and through the renewing of the Holy Spirit, whom He poured out on you abundantly through Jesus Christ our Saviour (Titus 3:5-6).

As you wash your body while living on earth, so you need to be washed and renewed in the inward man daily, lest you become blinded to God's blessed presence and ignorant of His great love.

What a wonderful Saviour we have in Jesus, who through the work of His grace continually keeps you washed in His precious blood!

Let's pray: Heavenly Father, thank You for the Holy Spirit who is working in my heart, cleansing me with the blood of Jesus so I can live in Your presence on earth.

In Jesus' name, Amen!

Who shall separate us from the love of Christ? Shall tribulation, or distress, or persecution, or famine, or nakedness, or peril, or sword?

Romans 8:35

What a wonderful comfort we have in Jesus, that He is always with us no matter what we are going through.

Many years ago, when I was pressed beyond measure and could not bear it any longer, I cried out, 'Help me Jesus! You must give me someone to stand with me. I am all alone!'

The Lord spoke to me and said, 'Until you learn to stand alone with me, I cannot add anyone to you.'

I shouted in praise, 'Jesus, You are more than enough for me!'

He said to me, 'Son, this battle is not yours, it is mine. I am with you.'

This is the grace of God in Christ Jesus - nothing or no one can separate you from His love. He is always with you to help you and bring you through whatever you are going through.

God Himself said, 'I will not in any way fail you nor give you up nor leave you without support. I will not, I will not, I will not in any degree leave you helpless nor forsake nor let you down (relax My hold on you) - assuredly not!'

So take comfort and be encouraged. Confidently and boldly say, 'The Lord is my helper; I will not be seized with alarm. I will not fear or dread or be terrified. What can man do to me?' (Hebrews 13:5-6 AMPB).

Now take some time and meditate on God's Word for it is written, 'I would have despaired and perished unless Your Word had been my deepest delight. I will never lay aside Your Word, for You have used them to restore my joy and health. I am Yours! Save me!' (Psalm 119:92-93 LB).

Let's pray: Heavenly Father, the love of Jesus is better to me than life itself. Therefore my lips will praise You and I will bless You because I know You are always with me. Speak to me as I open Your Word and show me wonderful things.

In Jesus' name, Amen!

He who did not spare His own Son, but delivered Him up for us all, how shall He not with Him also freely give us all things?
Romans 8:32

God demonstrated His own love for you in that while you were yet a sinner, Christ Jesus died for you. Now if He did so much for you while you were yet a sinner by dying for you, how much more will He do for you through His Life now you are His child!

You see in His death Jesus bore the pain and penalty of your sins so that through His Life He could bring forth in you your freedom from sin.

Would He who made provision in His death for you to have freedom in His Life with the Father, withhold any good thing from you?

Oh no, a thousand million times no!

Jesus Himself is God's guarantee that all the blessings He has with the Father are yours.

This is why Jesus is both Lord and Christ, so that He can assure your heart before God when you pray that whatever you ask in His Name He will do (John 14:14).

Therefore I say, let your heart rest in Him and come with confidence into God's presence.

Bring your requests before His throne of grace with the sweet joy of a child's expectation that whatever you ask in prayer you will receive (Mark 11:24).

Dear child of God, is there anything too hard for the Lord who made heaven and earth?

There is nothing He cannot do and there is no purpose that can be withheld from Him for He will freely give you all things.

So when you pray, believe that you are receiving the answers to your prayers.

Let's pray: Heavenly Father, You have made Jesus the guarantee that all He has with You in heaven is for me. I pray and believe You have given me to share in every good thing.

In Jesus' name, Amen!

At that day you will know that I am in My Father, and you in Me and I in you

John 14:20

Jesus is your access into God's presence. His Life is the Way into the Truth of God.

It is in that Life that He intercedes for you. In other words, this Life with the Father is what upholds and enables you to live in fellowship with the Father.

There is no room for doubt - Jesus lives in you. The clouds may be black and it may feel dark but the Life of Jesus is your light and salvation.

You may say, but what do I do when I feel lost and forsaken? Trust in Jesus! He is a wonderful Saviour; He will help you.

Daily delight yourself in Him, rejoice in Him and you will find your satisfaction and fulfillment in your communion with Him.

Jesus in you is what makes you brave, strong, and unafraid. Jesus is in you and is far greater and more powerful than sin, Satan, death or any problem you face.

Never forget you have Jesus to fight your battles, so lean your entire person on Him and you will see that through the work of His grace He will faithfully reveal His Life in you.

Remember how Paul and Silas were beaten and put in the darkest depths of a prison and held in chains. They did not allow themselves to be overcome by their circumstances but overcame, as at midnight they began to pray and sing hymns to God, while the other prisoners in the jail were listening to them. Then God brought about a great deliverance - the kind of deliverance He is working for you today (Acts 16.25).

You see this is the great miracle of it all, that the awesome God who made heaven and earth is with you and working on your behalf!

So take a moment and lift your holy hands and begin to pray and sing praises to Jesus.

As you do, the Life He has with the Father will flood your soul and make you whole.

Let's pray: Heavenly Father, You know what I am going through. I know Your mercies are new every morning. I worship You that the Life and love Jesus has with You in heaven is now also in me.
In Jesus' name, Amen!

I thank my God always concerning you for the grace of God which was given you by Christ Jesus, that you were enriched in everything by Him in all utterance and all knowledge

1 Corinthians 1:4-5

Just as the joy of a new born baby fills the heart of a parent, so it pleases God to see you enriched with all He has given Jesus at His throne. Be greatly encouraged, dear child of God, for He will give you every grace and blessing, every spiritual gift and enabling for doing His will during this time of waiting for the return of Jesus.

Do not let your heart become weary in doing well, for Jesus is with you and guarantees that you will be counted free from all sin and guilt on the day He returns. While this joy set before you is great, you are to rejoice in Him every day as He promises to enrich you with every good gift, so that in nothing you fall short of His glory, but in all you are, say and do, the Life He has with the Father is revealed in you.

You may say every good gift? Can I really expect God will give me every good gift?

Remember Jesus said, 'What man is there among you who, if his son asks for bread, will give him a stone? If you then, being evil, know how to give good gifts to your children, how much more will your Father who is in heaven give good things to those who ask Him?' (Matthew 7:9, 11-12).

This is the faith that pleases God - when you trust Him in everything and look to Him, radiant with expectation.

So put God's promises to the test and see how kind He is. See for yourself the way His mercies shower down on all who trust in Him. If you belong to Him, reverence Him; for everyone who does this has everything he needs. Trust in Jesus, be kind and good to others, and delight yourself in Him. Then He will give you all your heart's desires. Commit everything you do to Him. Trust Him to help you do it and He will. Rest in Jesus and wait patiently for Him to act, for those who trust in the Lord and humble themselves before Him shall be given every blessing, and shall have wonderful peace, for the Lord takes care of all those He has forgiven (Psalm 34 and 37 LB).

You see, you are now in His tender and loving care.

Jesus at the throne of God has full authority. He has the might and the right to shower heaven's blessings upon you.

Let's pray: Heavenly Father, I look to You, for I believe that in every area of my life You will enrich me so that in nothing I will fall short of Your glory.

In Jesus' name, Amen!

In that hour Jesus rejoiced in the Spirit and said, 'I thank You Father, Lord of heaven and earth, that You have hidden these things from the wise and prudent and revealed them to babes. Even so, Father, for so it seemed good in Your sight'

Luke 10:21

The saying, 'The joy of the Lord is my strength,' takes on a fresh, new meaning when you realise how pleased Jesus is to see you live in His power.

Begin to see Jesus rejoice over you that the power He has with Father is now working in you!

Perhaps you are like the disciples - still a babe in this Life that comes from above. Oh dear child of God, let the joy of the Lord encourage and strengthen you in the knowledge that Jesus is pleased to see you live in His power.

Don't be frustrated with yourself when there is still so much of His Life that needs to be developed in you. Remember, it is the work of His grace to draw you up into the Life He has with the Father. Believe you have received this Life and begin to share His goodness and grace with others.

Often at your lowest point, when you feel completely powerless and unable to help yourself, you receive an opportunity to do something good for another. This becomes a source of refreshing for you when in complete faith in Jesus you do what you can, and then begin to see Him do through you what you can't.

If you will but do the possible, then you will see Jesus do the impossible.

Most miracles follow an act of kindness. When Jesus was weary from His travels He rested by a well and met a woman whose life was restored as He talked with her. When Jesus saw God's power flow through Him giving her His heavenly Life, He said, 'This is My food, to do the will of My Father' (John 4:34). Jesus' strength was renewed as He experienced God's Life flowing through Him.

Let this encourage you to show kindness to anyone and thereby release God's power through you. Remember, as you do good Jesus will back you up with His power and His joy will become your strength.

Let's pray: Heavenly Father, I believe Your joy is to reveal the power Jesus has with You in heaven in me. Thank You for renewing my strength with Your joy.

In Jesus' name, Amen!

But of Him you are in Christ Jesus, who became for us wisdom from God - and righteousness, sanctification and redemption that as it is written, 'He who glories, let him glory in the Lord'
                                        1 Corinthians 1:30-31

When you begin to discover by His Spirit in you that Jesus has made you one with the Father in heaven, all you can do is glory in the amazing work of His grace.

The wisdom of Jesus' heavenly Life now flows through you - that divine virtue of God's favour in which He lives at the throne is in you, giving you His grace for good judgment and common sense.

This means you have His ability to make the right decision every time, knowing in every situation Jesus is directing your affairs and crowning your efforts with success. Jesus' wisdom guides your internal reasoning to live from above so that you have a steady flow of His goodness, resulting in only good deeds pouring forth from your life.

Because this wisdom comes from Jesus, it is first of all pure and full of quiet gentleness; it is peace-loving and courteous; it allows for discussion and is willing to yield to others because it is full of His mercy and kindness. This wisdom makes you tender-hearted and loving as it flows from His throne of grace. This wisdom is the meekness and humility of Jesus in you.

Jesus has become your righteousness, and in His righteousness you are given His sense of significance and self-worth in perfect right-standing with the Father. You know there is no charge against you; you know your record has been cleared because God Himself has declared you not guilty, holy and well pleasing in His sight.

You are sanctified, set apart through His heavenly Life in you; you are redeemed, purchased with the precious blood of Jesus, set free from the evil nature of sin!

So then, glory in the Lord because your life shines forth to the praise of the glory of His grace.

Every breath you take is a miracle of the work of His grace!

Let's pray: Heavenly Father, to You I give glory forever and ever because You placed me in Jesus Christ, in whom You have blessed me with every blessing He has with You in heaven.

In Jesus' name, Amen!

I am the vine, you are the branches. He who abides in Me, and I in him, bears much fruit; for without Me you can do nothing
John 15:5

Now that you are one with Jesus Christ at the throne of God, you will see the fruit of His heavenly Life in you. Others will see it too and begin to experience God's power through your Life in Him.

In October 1821, Charles G. Finney wrote about becoming one with Jesus and described it as an overwhelming baptism of the Holy Spirit. He said that it 'went right through me, as it seemed to me, body and soul. Immediately I found myself endued with such power from on high that a few words dropped here and there to individuals were the means of their immediate conversion. However sometimes I would find myself, in a great measure, empty of this power. I would then set apart a day for private fasting and prayer, fearing that this power had departed from me, and would inquire anxiously after the reason of this apparent emptiness. After humbling myself, and crying out for help, the power would return upon me with all its freshness. This has been the experience of my life.'

When Jesus says, 'without me you can do nothing,' He is saying that only through your union with Him are you able to share His heavenly blessings.

Learn therefore from the Holy Spirit, for He will help you cultivate a deep sense of hunger to abide in Jesus. He will teach you to draw your nourishment from Him.

The Holy Spirit will give you an unutterable sense of groaning and a deep burden to turn away from things that hinder your continual oneness with Jesus. The Holy Spirit yearns within you with a holy jealousy that you may share all the blessings Jesus has with the Father.

God does not want you to lose that sense of your oneness with Jesus for one split second, for He loves to see the fruit of His Life in you.

Let's pray: Heavenly Father, I humble my heart before You, for I know without Jesus I can do nothing. Thank You for keeping me one with Jesus. I need Your Holy Spirit to help me; teach me to abide in Him.

In Jesus' name, Amen!

*I am the vine, you are the braches. He who abides in Me, and
I in him, bears much fruit; for without Me you can do nothing*
John 15:5

When you hear Jesus say, 'without Me you can do nothing,' He
knows what that means because He said this even of Himself:
'The Son can do nothing of Himself, but what He sees the Father
do, the Father loves the Son, and shows Him all things that He
Himself does; and He will show Him greater works than these,
that you may marvel' (John 5:19-20).

Can you see how it pleased the Father to show Jesus what
to do?

This is how much He longs to bless you with every blessing so that
the Life Jesus has with the Father may flow through you like
a river.

You see, it was the Father in Jesus who enabled Him to do the
works that He did. And now Jesus says, 'because I go to the Father
you will be able to do the works I do' (John14:10-12).

Did you know that the riches of the glory of the Father's love
compels Jesus to reveal the wonders of His heavenly Life with all
its unlimited blessings in you?

Jesus wants to lift your tender heart of faith to see greater works.
There are greater things that He can do through you.

Consider what God was able to do through Jesus to bless the
whole world.

Now take off all the limits, for it is the joy of the Lord Jesus to do
the will of the Father and show you what to do!

Let's pray: Heavenly Father, my heart is overwhelmed with Your love; I know I can trust Jesus to work Your will in me so that I may share in all the blessings You have given Him and do the works You have prepared for me (Ephesians 2:10).

In Jesus' name, Amen!

As the Father loved Me, I also have loved you; abide in My love
John 15:9

To know that God is love, all you have to do is look to Jesus because He demonstrated the Father's love.

Too often we have all tried and failed to love others because we did not realise the powerful resource available to us by simply abiding in His love.

The love Jesus demonstrated astonished those who did not know that God is love.

A woman known to be a sinner came and wept, washing Jesus' feet with her tears and wiping them with her hair.

She then kissed His feet as she anointed them with a costly, aromatic oil.

While this was completely misunderstood by others, Jesus saw her heart of love and said, 'Her sins which are many are forgiven for she who loved much has been forgiven much. But to whom little is forgiven, the same loves little' (Luke 7:47).

When you abide in the love of Jesus you cannot but be overwhelmed by the fact that He has no charge against you, and that there is no condemnation in His heart because He has paid your debt in full with His own precious blood. He has borne all the pain of your shame. He believes in you and He really loves you!

Have you ever known such love - a love that drives out all fear?

Let the love of Jesus fill your heart and mind as a new beginning awaits you!

Oh yes, a whole new beginning was born in the heart of this woman as she entered into the love of Jesus. No one had ever loved her like this before; everyone had always seen her as a sinner, but Jesus looked at her with eyes of love and forgiveness.

It can be so painful to be misunderstood, rejected and seen to be a sinner. While many live in such a place of sorrow there is a place of grace where you may escape forever - it is the love of Jesus.

As you abide in His love, you will learn from Him to love others just as much as He loves you.

Let's pray: Heavenly Father, help me to abide in the love of Jesus and learn to love and forgive like Him.

In Jesus' name, Amen!

What then shall we say to these things? If God is for us, who can be against us?

Romans 8:31

When you look into the mirror, do you admire God's handiwork and say to Him, 'I will praise You, for I am fearfully and wonderfully made! Marvelous are Your works, and that my soul knows very well' (Psalm 139:14).

You must realise that you are predestined to be conformed to His image (Genesis 1:26). This is why God called you into fellowship with Jesus, so that He can transform you into His likeness (2 Corinthians 3:18).

Think about this, the Life Jesus has with the Father in heaven is what He now gives to you.

What then shall we say in response to this?

If God is for you, who can be against you? He who did not spare His own Son, but gave Him up for you, how will He not graciously give you all things with Him? Who will bring a charge against you, when God Himself has justified you? Who will condemn you, when Jesus paid such a high price for you in His death and in His Life at the throne of God where He lives to intercede for you to impart the Life and blessings He has with the Father?

Now you know no matter what you're going through, nothing can ever separate you from the love of the Father!

No trouble, suffering or persecution can ever make you think that God does not love you! No, quite the opposite! In all this you know you are more than a conqueror through Him who loves you and who freely gives and maintains in you the Life He has given to Jesus.

Oh, what comfort to know that neither death nor life, neither the angels nor demons, neither the past, present or future, nor any power, nor anything else in all creation, will ever be able to separate you from the love of the Father! (Romans 8:31-39).

So take comfort and be encouraged and confidently and boldly say, 'The Lord is my Helper; I will not be seized with alarm [I will not fear or dread or be terrified]. What can man do to me? (Psalm 27:1; 118:6; Hebrews 13:6 AMPB).

Let's pray: Heavenly Father, I know You love me. I know You are with me. I know nothing can separate me from Your love. Nothing can defeat me. I love You, Father; You are my strength and song, my invincible army.

In Jesus' name, Amen!

As you therefore have received Christ Jesus the Lord, so walk in Him, rooted and built up in Him and established in the faith, as you have been taught, abounding in it with thanksgiving

Colossians 2:6-7

Just as you trusted Jesus to save you, you can trust Him for each day's problems because He lives in you.

As you discover the resources available to you in Jesus, you will never stop singing His praises. Your faith will keep growing as you plant your roots deep in His love for you. Learn to draw your strength from Him and you will discover your ability is what He works through you.

When you walk by your own ability you will always end up limiting God. But to walk in Jesus is to have His ability become yours.

When Jesus is your ability you can face anything and know no matter what happens, you can do all things through Christ who strengthens you (Philippians 4:13).

The Apostle Paul said, 'I would never dare think anything comes from myself, for my ability is what God works through me' (2 Corinthians 3:5).

This is the joy of walking in Him - Jesus enables you to live as He lives, to have what He has, and to do what He does.

What an adventure to be a Christian and walk in Jesus!

As it is written, 'The steps of a good man are ordered by the Lord, and He delights in His way' (Psalm 37:23).

Be of good courage, dear child of God, Jesus is with you in every step you take.

Let's pray: Heavenly Father, I thank You for loving me and showing me how to walk through each day with Your ability.

In Jesus' name, Amen!

Then Jesus answered and said to them, 'Most assuredly, I say to you, the Son can do nothing of Himself, but what He sees the Father do; for whatever He does, the Son also does in like manner'

John 5:19

What wonderful confidence comes from knowing that your ability is what God works through you! It takes away the fear of failure and fills your heart with faith.

When Moses drew back from the task of going to deliver God's people from bondage - because he felt insecure and unable to speak - God said, 'Have I not made your mouth, can I not enable you to speak. Go, and I will be with your mouth and teach you what you shall say' (Exodus 4:12). Now see this humble shepherd in his weakness made strong by the power of God to face the mightiest nation on earth and bring forth God's people with joy, just as God said, and on the very day He planned.

There is really nothing too difficult for the Lord to accomplish if He has the right person to do it with. All through Scripture you can see how God enables those who trust in Him.

It was no different for Jesus. When He returned to His home town of Nazareth in the power of the Holy Spirit, He read words from Isaiah: 'The Spirit of the Lord is upon me, because He has anointed me to preach the gospel to the poor; He has sent me to heal the broken-hearted, to proclaim liberty to the captives and recovery of sight to the blind, to set at liberty those who are oppressed; to proclaim the acceptable year of the Lord.' And He said, 'Today this scripture is fulfilled in your hearing' (Luke 4:14-21). All who heard Jesus say this were in awe because of the grace that proceeded from Him.

You see God desires His word to be fulfilled in you. He longs to enable you with His ability to live a truly godly life. This means

He will enable you to be a good husband, father, wife, mother, son, or daughter. Yes, He will give you everything you need to build a happy, healthy home.

He will enable you in the workplace, or any other area of life, so all can see by the grace that proceeds from you that God is your Father and you are His child.

Let's pray: Heavenly Father, I know You love me. I trust You to enable me so all may see I am Your child.

In Jesus' name, Amen!

Love has been perfected among us in this: that we may have boldness in the day of judgment; because as He is, so are we in this world

1 John 4:17

What amazing grace, that Jesus in heaven empowers you to live like Him on earth!

Let the truth of Jesus' immeasurable love deeply penetrate your heart and take away all uncertainty of what will happen on the Day of Judgment.

Remember, Jesus showed you God's plan for salvation. He is the one who made you acceptable to God. He is the one who gave you a new heart and mind, with right desires and godly thoughts. Yes, Jesus made you pure and holy as surely as He gave Himself to purchase your salvation.

Jesus said, 'Most assuredly, I say to you, he who hears My word and believes in Him who sent Me has everlasting life, and shall not come into judgment, but has passed from death into life' (John 5:24).

You have His life in you keeping you in fellowship with the Father. So instead of fear you now live by faith in Jesus and rejoice in the hope that when you see Him you will be just like Him, radiant with His glory (Colossians 3:4).

The Lord Jesus Himself guarantees that you will be counted free from all sin and guilt on the Day of Judgment.

Therefore give thanks to God for all the wonderful gifts He gives.

He has enriched your whole life now that you belong to Jesus.

You are given every grace and blessing and every spiritual gift and power for doing His will, while you are waiting for His return.

Follow the example of Jesus and live as He lives!

Let's pray: Heavenly Father, I know You have given me everything for living like Jesus. I know You love me and will present me blameless before You on the Day of Judgment. I know I will shine to the praise of the glory of Your grace.

In Jesus' name, Amen!

But when it pleased God, who separated me from my mother's womb and called me through His grace

Galatians 1:15

God was pleased to see you born and call you by His grace. Even before He made heaven and earth, He planned to make you His very own child through what Jesus would do for you. Now it is His great joy to call you by His grace, because of His great love.

Can you see how very much the Heavenly Father loves you? He allows you to be called His child. Think of it, you really are His child! (1 John 3:1).

From now on God can always point to you as an example of how very rich His kindness is in all He has done for you through Jesus Christ (Ephesians 2:7).

You see, the grace, the loving-kindness and goodness by which you are called a child of God are more wonderful than the human mind can comprehend.

Jesus rejoices that with every breath you take, the life you now live is lived to the praise of the glory of His grace.

When I was a child I often heard my mother sing, 'It is well with my soul.' This song is etched deep within my heart, especially now that I have become a child of God.

Oh, how the wonder of His love and grace restores your soul and makes you whole! He leaves nothing undone. He makes everything good. He beautifies you with His holiness and perfects you in His righteousness. He quiets you with His peace and fills you with Himself until your entire spirit, soul and body are filled and flooded with God Himself.

God the Father delights in you!

Let the refreshing of His presence fill your heart anew.

Begin to sing, 'It is well with my soul!'

Let's pray: Heavenly Father, it is well with my soul. Because Your loving-kindness is better than life, my lips shall praise You. I will bless You while I live. I will lift up my hands to the praise of the glory of Your grace. (Psalm 63:3-5)

In Jesus' name, Amen!

When peace like a river, attendeth my way,
When sorrows like sea billows roll;
Whatever my lot, Thou hast taught me to say,
It is well, it is well, with my soul.

Refrain:
It is well, (it is well),
With my soul, (with my soul)
It is well, it is well, with my soul.

Though Satan should buffet, though trials should come,
Let this blest assurance control,
That Christ has regarded my helpless estate,
And hath shed His own blood for my soul.

My sin — oh, the bliss of this glorious thought! —
My sin — not in part but the whole, —
Is nailed to the cross, and I bear it no more,
Praise the Lord, praise the Lord, O my soul!

For me, be it Christ, be it Christ hence to live:
If Jordan above me shall roll,
No pang shall be mine, for in death as in life,
Thou wilt whisper Thy peace to my soul.

But Lord, 'tis for Thee, for Thy coming we wait,
The sky, not the grave, is our goal;
Oh, trump of the angel! Oh, voice of the Lord!
Blessed hope, blessed rest of my soul.

And Lord, haste the day when my faith shall be sight,
The clouds be rolled back as a scroll;
The trump shall resound, and the Lord shall descend,
Even so, it is well with my soul

Horatio G. Spafford, 1873.

If we walk in the light as He is in the light, we have fellowship with one another, and the blood of Jesus Christ His Son cleanses us from all sin

1 John 1:7

To walk in the light means you are living the Life Jesus has with the Father.

Living in the light is wonderful; it is the sweet communion of the Son with the Father. This Life knows no sin or separation from the love of the Father. This Life is in you to the praise of Him who called you out of darkness into His marvelous light (1 Peter 2:9).

There are not enough words to describe how wonderful it is to live in the light of His presence and enjoy the Life and love Jesus has with the Father.

Jesus prayed, 'Father, I will keep on revealing You so that the mighty love You have for Me may be in them, and I in them' (John 17:26).

Just as the sun shines from heaven upon you, so the glory of the Life Jesus has with the Father is shining on you, unhindered and forever.

Dear child of God, even if things seem dark around you and confusion tries to blind you, don't be afraid. Don't be dismayed, for though once your heart was full of darkness, now it is full of light from the Lord Jesus. Learn as you go along what pleases Him and have no fellowship with the unfruitful works of darkness (Ephesians 5:8).

Jesus is the light of God's Life in you, so look to Him and you will become radiant with His Life and will see the light of His glory streaming from you.

Now say this out loud:

'The Lord is my light and my salvation; whom shall I fear? The Lord is the strength of my life; of whom shall I be afraid?' (Psalm 27:1).

Let's pray: Heavenly Father, You are my light and my salvation, whom shall I fear - of whom shall I be afraid. You are the light of my life. My heart is filled with Your glory.

In Jesus' name, Amen!

If we walk in the light as He is in the light, we have fellowship with one another, and the blood of Jesus Christ His Son cleanses us from all sin

1 John 1:7

When you think of the cleansing of your sins, the Scriptures do not leave you guessing as to what that means. From the moment sin entered the human race - and thereby death spread to everyone - we see that God's gift of forgiveness comes only through Jesus.

When John the Baptist saw Jesus coming toward him he said, 'Behold the Lamb of God who takes away the sin of the world!' (John 1:29).

Jesus did not come to *cover* our sins, as the blood of the sacrificial lamb had under the old covenant, but He came to *take away* the deepest stain of sin through the power of His precious blood.

I pray that the revelation of the cleansing flood of Christ's blood lives in your heart!

You see when Jesus died and rose again, He established the cleansing of your sins in His own blood. Having fully cleared your record of every charge He sat down at the right hand of God. He now reigns from heaven to pour out His Spirit on you. And the Holy Spirit is at work in your heart with the blood of Jesus to cleanse you from the power and consciousness of sin so that you can enjoy living in the light of God's presence, where Jesus is, without ever having to feel guilty or ashamed.

Once you were lost in sin but God longed to be merciful to you to satisfy the great love He feels for you. So even though you were spiritually dead in your sins He made you alive with Jesus.

Can you see that you have been saved by grace through the great mercies of God?

Think about the wonder of the salvation the Father has given to you - the Life Jesus has with Him in heaven. Now you can have real faith for His Life is in you. This is the work of His grace. So there is nothing to boast about except Jesus, to whom belongs everlasting praise for giving you a share in the new creation of the Life He has with the Father.

Let's pray: Heavenly Father, I am a new creation, no more in condemnation, here in Your grace I stand, for You have cleansed me from all my sins. You have cleared my record and removed every charge against me through the precious blood of Jesus. I love You Lord and I lift my hands as I give You praise.

In Jesus' name, Amen!

As the living Father sent Me, and I live because of the Father, so he who feeds on Me will live because of Me

John 6:57

The amazing Life Jesus lived came to Him from His Father in heaven.

Just as hunger for food gives you the feeling that you must eat something, so the Holy Spirit yearns within you for fellowship with Jesus, for only He can satisfy. He is the bread of life. He said, 'If you come to Me you shall never hunger and if you believe in Me you shall never thirst' (John 6:35).

Out of the fullness of the Life Jesus has with the Father, you will receive one grace after another - spiritual blessing upon spiritual blessing, even favour upon favour and gift upon gift (John 1:16 AMPB).

This is why Jesus taught us to pray, 'Our Father who is in heaven, give us this day our daily bread.'

You see, Jesus is the bread of heaven! The Life He has with the Father is what enables you to live and become utterly satisfied with His love.

You know that when you eat natural food you will hunger again; so it is with your fellowship with Jesus. Today you are filled and flooded with His glory; tomorrow you can wake up and feel it's gone, but don't ever think that. For even as the sun pours forth light and heat, so your Heavenly Father supplies your every need, according to His riches and glory by Christ Jesus (Philippians 4:19).

As we sing in that beautiful hymn, 'Great is Your faithfulness, oh God my Father, morning by morning new mercies I see. All I have needed Your hand has provided; great is Your faithfulness, Lord unto me!'

So come and feast yourself on the Life Jesus has with the Father.

Let's pray: Heavenly Father, the eyes of all mankind look up to You for help. You give them their food as they need it. You constantly satisfy the hunger and thirst of every living thing (Psalm 145:15-16 LB). I worship You because You satisfy me with the Life Jesus has with You in heaven.

In Jesus' name, Amen!

Great is Thy faithfulness, O God my Father.
There is no shadow of turning with Thee;
Thou changest not, Thy compassions they fail not;
As Thou has been Thou forever wilt be.

Great is Thy faithfulness! Great is Thy faithfulness!
Morning by morning new mercies I see;
All I have needed Thy hand hath provided;
Great is Thy faithfulness, Lord, unto me!

Summer and winter, and springtime and harvest,
Sun, moon, and stars in their courses above,
Join with all nature in manifold witness,
To Thy great faithfulness, mercy, and love.

Great is Thy faithfulness! Great is Thy faithfulness!
Morning by morning new mercies I see;
All I have needed Thy hand hath provided;
Great is Thy faithfulness, Lord, unto me!

Pardon for sin and a peace that endureth,
Thy own dear presence to cheer and to guide;
Strength for today and bright hope for tomorrow,
Blessings all mine, with ten thousand beside!

Great is Thy faithfulness! Great is Thy faithfulness!
Morning by morning new mercies I see;
All I have needed Thy hand hath provided;
Great is Thy faithfulness, Lord, unto me!

Thomas Obediah Chisholm, 1923.

He answered and said to them, 'Because it has been given to you to know the mysteries of the kingdom of heaven, but to them it has not been given'

Matthew 13:11

Things that have been hidden for generations have now been made manifest through Jesus. It is in Him we see the Word made flesh. All God spoke that He longed for man to enjoy we now see revealed in Jesus.

The prophets of old spoke by the Spirit of Christ of our wonderful salvation. They longed to understand these things as they spoke about Christ's suffering and the glory that followed. They understood that God was speaking of things to come (1 Peter 1:10-12).

Through the ages the Scriptures have served as a guiding light to lead all people to Jesus Christ, who is the fulfillment of our God given hope.

God has given you the Holy Spirit through Jesus to open your eyes and ears and enlighten your heart to all He has freely given you in Him.

For every promise of God is 'yes' in Jesus, and because of His Life in you, you can say Amen (so be it) to the glory of God (2 Corinthians 1:20).

It has now been given to you to know the mysteries of the kingdom of heaven, where Jesus is seated at the right hand of God ever-living to make intercession for you so that you may share the Life He has with the Father.

Dear child of God, Jesus holds nothing back. He is the door; He is the way; it is through Him all God's promises come to pass in you.

What a glorious Life you have in Jesus; kings and prophets desired to see what you see, yet they all died in the faith that they would be heirs of the same promises.

Consider how rich you are in Jesus, that you have become partakers of His Life.

Now enjoy living in the freedom and power He has with the Father.

Let's pray: Heavenly Father, for all the glory You have given me to share in Jesus, I give You praise. You have opened the Scriptures to me through Jesus and the blessings of His heavenly Life. I love You, Father!

In Jesus' name, Amen!

Nevertheless when one turns to the Lord, the veil is taken away
2 Corinthians 3:16

The glory of God was shining from Moses when he came down from the mountain after having talked with God face to face (Exodus 34:30). In this God gave a foretaste of what He now gives to you in Jesus. For even though it was a fading reflection of God's glory on the face of Moses, this same light of Life has now been given to shine in your heart (2 Corinthians 4:6).

Why did Moses put a veil over His face when the Light of God shone from him? It was because the people could not endure seeing the glory while there was sin in their hearts.

Why is the veil taken away when you turn to Jesus? It is because He has come to take away your sins by filling you with His Life.

Therefore you are given to reflect His light, not as Moses from whom the glory faded, but as the Son of God in glory. You will shine brighter and brighter until that soon coming Day when you see Jesus and will be transformed in the twinkling of an eye and made perfect in His likeness.

There will be no veiled faces then when you see Him, no tears of shame or pain of guilt, but only the joy of the redeemed, for you will see Him and be just like Him (1 John 3:2).

Dear child of God, look to Jesus. He is your ever-living Hope of glory.

His Spirit in you removes the veil when you read or hear His Word because there is no more pain of shame, or guilt of sin, but only the assurance that the glory of His heavenly Life that awaits you in His presence is already living in your heart.

You are a witness of Jesus!

Jesus at the throne of God is Jesus in you!

Let's pray: Heavenly Father, I thank You for removing the veil through the Spirit of Jesus in me so that I may boldly make Him known in all I am, say and do!

In Jesus' name, Amen!

Jesus said to him, 'Have I been with You so long, and yet You have not known Me, Philip? He who has seen Me has seen the Father; so how can You say, 'Show us the Father'?'

John 14:9

What image do you bear as a child of God? This is to be no mystery, for Jesus has shown you in Himself the image to which you are called to be conformed (Romans 8:29).

You see before you turned to Jesus you knew no other image than your own and that was not sufficient to feed your sense of worth. Perhaps you have been seeking for the real you. It is quite amazing what image people will pursue.

But this is the wonder of Jesus, He helps you find the real you in God.

Oh, how wonderful it is when the beautiful rays of God's glory begin to shine in your heart so that when you look in the mirror you begin to love yourself as God loves you.

Jesus never suffered with His self-worth, rather the opposite. He said, 'He who has seen Me has seen the Father.'

Just as Moses bore the radiant glory of the image of God, so you bear the image of Jesus who is the image of God. This is why you will never have to suffer that awful pain of shame again, or feel insecure in the presence of any other person, no matter what you look like. For the Life you now live is the Life of Jesus who loves you and gave Himself for you.

Think on this whenever you are trying to overcome feelings that threaten your worth or make you feel inferior to others.

Never compare yourself to anyone else but Jesus, for He alone is the mirror of truth who reflects perfectly the real you.

You may say, but this is my sorrow, when I look at Him I still feel so human. Oh dearly beloved, have you not heard? This is exactly why Jesus came, not to blame you and make you feel ashamed, but to save you and fill you with the love He has with the Father.

The more you look to Jesus and receive Him, the more you become like Him.

Now let this revelation deeply penetrate your heart and mind, not only to restore your sense of worth, but to give you His identity as a child of God.

Let's pray: Heavenly Father, You know who I am. I trust You to help me look to Jesus so I can clearly see my true identity and realise how much You love me. Father, I want others to see You when they see me.

In Jesus' name, Amen!

As the Father knows Me, even so I know the Father; and I lay down My life for the sheep

John 10:15

Perhaps the greatest wonder in living from above is that the same Spirit that filled Jesus when He was baptised has come to live in you, so that even as Jesus heard God say, 'You are My beloved Son; in You I am well pleased,' so you may know for yourself who your Heavenly Father is and His great love for you.

To know who you are you need to know that God is your Father. Can you see the wonder of the beautiful Life Jesus came to bring? A Life that came forth from the Father, a Life in perfect harmony with Him.

There is no lack in the Father's love for you; it is His delight to reveal that you are His child. This is why Jesus said, 'I am ascending to My Father and your Father and to My God and your God' (John 20:17). Let this wonderful truth fill and flood your soul. God is your Father, you are His child! The Life you have received is the Life of God, the same Life by which Jesus is the Son of God. This Life in you proves that Jesus bought you with His own precious blood and set you free from the power of sin and death. It confirms that the Father loves you as much as He loves Jesus.

Take a moment and meditate on this truth, and then let your praise rise to Jesus your Saviour and God your Father. Through the Spirit of God in you, you are being transformed as you learn to think and talk like Jesus. This is how Jesus talked:

'My Father loves Me. I am in My Father and My Father is in Me. My Father and I are one. If you have seen Me you have seen My Father. I can do nothing of Myself except what I see My Father do. The Father is always with Me for I always do the things that please Him.'

When you look at Jesus you see He had no life outside of His relationship with the Father. He saw everything from His Father's perspective. He never talked about Himself unless it was what His Father thought of Him. He never did anything except what His Father showed Him.

To live this way may seem impossible for you, but this is exactly why Jesus lives in you. Now look into the mirror with a big smile and say, 'I love You Jesus for loving me!'

Let's pray: Heavenly Father, You sent Jesus so I can know who You are and so I can begin to see who I am. Thank You for giving me Your Spirit and making me Your child.

In Jesus' name, Amen!

Jesus answered and said to him, 'Blessed are you, Simon Bar-Jonah for flesh and blood has not revealed this to you, but My Father in heaven'

Matthew 16:17

With Christ at the throne of God is all about knowing the Life Jesus has with the Father and learning to live from above.

Often what makes our lives complicated is when we lean on our own understanding and look at things from our perspective. There are many who have turned away from their true destiny - even when they had travelled so far and were so near to it - because they could not see the way ahead and gave up hope. This is why on the old ships people built a crow's nest at the top of the main mast, where a man could look and see beyond what others were able to see below.

There are so many things we have available today to help us see. Satellites surround the globe providing navigation for our daily use - something unthinkable for the man who climbed the crow's nest. Should it then be so unthinkable that Jesus at the throne of God will help you navigate through life? When Moses brought the children of Israel from Egypt through the terrible wilderness to the land given them by God, he was given a column of fire by night and a cloud by day to show the way.

In 1951, my father wrote a letter to my mother when he was sailing the seven seas as a cook on a big ship. The Scripture he put at the top of his letter left a deep impression on me when my mother showed me this letter some years ago. 'I will instruct you and teach you in the way you should go; I will guide you with my eye' (Psalm 32:8). God knows the way ahead and it is His delight to order your steps. Even if you were to fall He will say, 'Don't give up. I will lift you up. I will help you.'

For Simon Bar-Jonah, who is also called Peter, his destiny became clear when God in heaven revealed to him that Jesus is the Christ, the Son of living God. Peter left everything to follow Jesus. While before he was but a fisherman, when he started to follow Jesus he became the big fisher of men, the mighty Apostle of Christ and a worker of miracles. His confession that Jesus was the Son of God became the rock and revelation on which Jesus could build His church.

This is the joy you have in Jesus at the throne of God - that He is there to guide you down here, so you will never need to give up hope that your destiny is secure.

Let's pray: Heavenly Father, You know the way I go. You know the thoughts of my heart. I trust You to guide me by Your Spirit.
In Jesus' name, Amen!

To my Darling Willeke.
From your Johnny.
Le Havre 22 Nov. 1951. France.
Ps. 32:8.

Let this mind be in you
which was also in Christ Jesus!

A dedicated spirit is:
Wholy given to God
To know Him,
To choose His will.
To resemble His character.
To trust His word.
To love Him supremely
To glorify Him only
To enjoy Him wholly
And to belong to Him utterly,
unreservedly and forever!

Surrender
It means separation.
It means sacrifice.
It means self denial.
It means death.
Surrender is giving up self.
a yielding to God voluntary,
to lay our whole life on the altar.
Christian life is a Christ life.
It is not a immitation.
But a incarnation.

And He said to them, 'You are from beneath; I am from above. You are of this world; I am not of this world'

John 8:23

Jesus came down from heaven and appeared among us as a man. He gladly gave up His mighty power and glory as God and clothed Himself in human flesh to reveal the Life He has with the Father. He said, 'The Life I live is not of this world.'

Just as the different cultures throughout the world have beautiful distinguishing qualities that set them apart, even so it is unmistakable to see God's glory in the Life of Jesus.

Now when you are born from above with God's divine nature you are not of this world any more than Jesus. This world is not your eternal home; you are only passing through, for your citizenship is in heaven where you are a member of God's household.

Jesus said, 'I know where I come from and where I am going.' For Him heaven was not some imaginary place but His eternal home. Heaven is a real place - no less real than the Promised Land was for the children of Israel. Even as they lived in tents until they entered their inheritance promised to Abraham, so you live in a temporal body until you enter your inheritance in the light of God's presence and are given a new body.

So now that you have this hope, live in such a way that while at home in the body you shine forth with the light of the Life of Jesus.

Jesus spoke of His heavenly Life in you as a lamp that lights up the whole house and is clear for everyone to see. Therefore let the light of His Life so shine that all may see, by the love and kindness you have for others, that God is your Father and that you are well pleasing to Him.

Be imitators of God as dear children (Ephesians 5:1)!

Let's pray: Heavenly Father, I know the Life You have given me is the Life Jesus has with You in heaven. I am not of this world any more than Jesus is. I pray that the light of Your Life is clear for all to see.

In Jesus' Name, Amen.

Therefore if the Son makes you free, you shall be free indeed
John 8:36

It is hard to imagine without experiencing it what true freedom looks like. When Nicodemus came to Jesus he acknowledged God was with Him because of the miracles Jesus did. Jesus told Nicodemus, if you truly want to see the kingdom of God in your life you must be born again (John 3:3).

What Jesus was saying to Nicodemus was that intellectual knowledge of the things of God is not enough. You must be born again.

Nicodemus had to have a spiritual birth to be able to live the Life he saw in Jesus.

Only then could he truly understand the things of God and enjoy His blessings in life.

When Jesus said, 'Whom the Son makes free is free indeed,' He was talking about setting you free to live the Life you see in Him.

You see, you are born into freedom - the freedom of God's children, and because you are His child you have become an heir of the Life Jesus has with the Father.

You are no longer a stranger to God or a foreigner to heaven, but you are a member of the family; you belong in God's household with every other Christian (Ephesians 2:19).

Think about this, God gives you His Spirit so you may know He is your Father. True freedom is the Life of Jesus in your heart crying, 'Abba Father, I love You!'

For Jesus, freedom was living life in the love of the Father, being of one heart and mind with Him, sharing the same Spirit. Jesus loved doing the will of the Father and the Father loved being with Jesus, giving Him whatever He asked.

This is the freedom Jesus gives; the Life He has in the Father's love.

You cannot imagine how wonderful this freedom is until His Spirit fills your heart and you begin to taste and see that the Lord is good!

Let's pray: Heavenly Father, to You belong the kingdom, the power and the glory forever. Thank You for giving me freedom to live in Your love here on earth.

In Jesus' Name, Amen.

And since your old sin-loving nature 'died' with Christ, we know that you will share His Life

Romans 6:8 (LB)

One of the greatest discoveries you can make through Jesus Christ is that when He died on the cross, He took on Himself your old sin-loving nature and destroyed its power in His death.

When Jesus died, the sin nature died in Him once and for all. When God raised Jesus, He declared Him to be His Son by the Spirit of Holiness through the resurrection of the dead (Romans 1:4).

Perhaps you did not know this, but because Adam sinned, death entered the human race (Romans 5:12).

Can you see how powerful the sin-nature is, that because Adam sinned all died because of him?

Can you also see how powerful the righteousness of Jesus is, that because He fully obeyed God, conquering sin, hell and death, you can now live the Life He lives – a Life free from sin?

Free from the power of sin and death, Jesus now gives you the Life He has with the Father. There is therefore no more room for doubt, sin is no longer your master, you are no longer its slave. You are a child of God! You have a new master so to speak; the Life Jesus has with the Father now reigns in you.

You may ask yourself, but how does this work? Well, when you did not know the Life of Jesus in you, you were helpless and gave yourself over to whatever your human nature desired. But now that you have His Life in you, He enables you to live free from sin through His Life. He empowers you to be full of His goodness and love so that you are now able to do kind and good things for others that show you are a child of God.

So put all your trust in Jesus and don't ever be afraid of your old master sin again; he has nothing in you for Jesus now lives in you!

Let's pray: Heavenly Father, thank You for giving me the Life Jesus has with You, so that I may live free from sin and enjoy sweet fellowship with You.

In Jesus' Name, Amen.

But now having been set free from sin, and having become slaves of God, you have your fruit to holiness, and the end, everlasting life

Romans 6:22

It is true there is forgiveness with God (Psalm 130:4) and that is wonderful.

But there is more, there is a life free from sin through the power of Jesus Christ within.

But then there is even much more, as you begin to partake of the Life Jesus has with the Father you will start seeing the fruit of His holiness fill your life.

And then the end of it all, oh what glory and joy, there is eternal life in His presence!

When Isaiah saw the glory of God and heard the angels cry, 'Holy, holy, holy is the Lord of hosts; the whole earth is full of His glory!' Isaiah cried, 'Woe is me, for I am undone, because I have unclean lips; for my eyes have seen the King, the Lord of hosts.'

Sometimes we don't realise how far separated we live from the glory and holiness of God until we have an experience like Isaiah did.

However, God does not desire this to be a temporary experience but your daily bread. He longs for you to feed on the Life Jesus has with the Father every day. He wants you to experience the fruit of His holiness continually.

God touched Isaiah's lips with the fire of His holiness and he became a different man – a man who dared to speak for God.

Today, God is here to touch your lips with the fire of His holiness and give you the power of His Son Jesus to speak for Him and turn the heart of your nation to see a mighty revival of love for God.

Let's pray: Heavenly Father, I pray that the earth will be filled with Your glory! I pray that the hearts of people will melt with love for You as I speak of Your goodness. Thank You for forgiving me and filling me with Your heavenly, holy Life.

In Jesus' Name, Amen.

Even the righteousness of God, through faith in Jesus Christ, to all and on all who believe

Romans 3:22

When you think of righteousness, what do you think that means? Someone has defined it as, 'The ability to stand in God's presence without any sense of failure, guilt or shame.' Sure, that is true! But how can you ever rise to such heights of purity when even Moses covered his face as he stood on holy ground?

I love the heart of the Psalmist who said, 'My mouth shall tell of Your righteousness and Your salvation all the day, for I do not know their limits. I will go in the strength of the Lord God; I will make mention of Your righteousness, of Yours only!' (Psalm 71:15-16).

To worship God for His righteousness is great, but to see Him impart that same righteousness into your heart is greater still; it is an indescribable gift – one that lifts your soul to heaven's throne of grace so that your whole life shines forth to God's praise.

Consider the Apostle Paul as he discovered this indescribable lavish gift. He said, 'As far as keeping the Jewish Law is concerned, I was a Pharisee. As far as a person can be righteous by obeying the commands of the Law, I was without fault. But all those things that I might count as profit I now reckon as loss for Christ's sake. Not only those things; I reckon everything as complete loss for the sake of what is so much more valuable, the knowledge of Christ Jesus my Lord. For His sake I have thrown everything away; I consider it all as mere rubbish, so that I may gain Christ and be completely united with Him. I no longer have a righteousness of my own, the kind that is gained by obeying the Law. I now have the righteousness that is given through faith in Jesus, the righteousness that comes from God and is based on faith' (Philippians 3:4-9 GNB).

It is because Jesus took your sins in His own body on the cross that God does not impute your trespasses to you. And it is because God raised Jesus from the dead that He freely imparts His own righteousness to you. Only because of the glory of Jesus' accomplished work can you stand in God's presence and experience His peace - a peace which is far more wonderful than the human mind can comprehend - and have the true joy of knowing that the righteousness Jesus has with the Father is in you by His Spirit.

Let's pray: Heavenly Father, how great Thou art! Then sings my soul, my Saviour God to Thee, how great Thou art! You have cleared my record and given me Your own righteousness. How great Thou art!

In Jesus' Name, Amen.

For if when we were enemies we were reconciled to God through the death of His Son, much more, having been reconciled, we shall be saved by His life

Romans 5:10

If God has done so much for you through the death of His Son while you were yet a sinner, how much more will He do for you through the Life of His Son now that you are His child.

You see it pleases the Father that you believe He has taken away all your sins through the death of His Son Jesus. What is more, the Father did all this so that through the resurrection you might live the life Jesus has with Him in heaven.

Please remember this: God did not merely save you FROM something, He also saved you TO something. If the death of Jesus Christ rescues us from sin and death, the resurrection of Jesus Christ empowers us to live the Life that He has with the Father. God saved you so that you might be able to live the Life He has given Jesus at His right hand.

This is why Jesus is the author of your faith.

The faith I am talking about here is the faith Jesus has with the Father in heaven.

Everything you need is found in the Life that Jesus has with the Father. He will fill you with His loving, trusting, perfect faith in God. The more you come to know Jesus, the more you will experience this perfect faith.

So if you want more of God's kindness and peace, then learn to know Jesus better. For as you know Him He will give you, through the Life He has with the Father, everything for living a truly godly Life. He will even share His own glory, His own character and goodness with you, to keep you free from all the lust and corruption of sin. He will bless you richly and grant you increasing freedom from all anxiety and fear. Jesus will fill you with all of Himself until you know through experience for yourself the Life He has with the Father.

All honour belongs to God, the Father of the Lord Jesus Christ, for through His boundless mercy He has given you the privilege to be born again and be His child.

I pray that God our Father will receive great glory because of the Life of His Son Jesus in you.

Let's pray: Heavenly Father, I am so grateful to be born again with the Life Jesus has with You in heaven. You are so kind and good to me!

In Jesus' Name, Amen.

There is therefore now no condemnation to those who are in Christ Jesus, who do not walk according to the flesh, but according to the Spirit

Romans 8:1

I hear the song of the redeemed in heaven, 'Salvation belongs to our God who sits on the throne, and to the Lamb,' sung by countless saints who have reaped the sweet fruit of their faith in Jesus and stand before His throne (Revelation 7:10).

When you seek peace with God through faith in Jesus, you will never have to suffer that horrible pain of condemnation again.

As the old hymns so powerfully remind us, 'Before the throne of God above, I have a strong and perfect plea, a great High Priest whose Name is love, who ever lives and pleads for me. My name is graven on His hands, my name is written on His heart, I know that while in heaven He stands, no tongue can bid me thence depart, no tongue can bid me thence depart.'

'When Satan tempts me to despair and tells me of the guilt within, upward I look and see Him there, who made an end to all my sin. Because the sinless Saviour died, my sinful soul is counted free, for God, the Just, is satisfied, to look on Him and pardon me, to look on Him and pardon me.'

Oh, I can't help myself; I must add the last verse!

'Behold Him there the risen lamb, my perfect spotless righteousness, the great unchangeable I AM, the King of glory and of grace. One with Himself, I cannot die, my soul is purchased with His blood; my life is hid with Christ on high, with Christ my Saviour and my God, with Christ my Saviour and my God.'

Who would want to build on such sinking sand as their own ability to find peace with God? No, never look to your own ability, but rejoice in Christ Jesus for the Life He has with the Father now lives in you.

His Life in you guarantees your unbroken fellowship with the Father.

Come dearly beloved, and give yourself entirely to Jesus; His loving grace will keep you free forever from the pain of condemnation.

Let's pray: Heavenly Father, I love You for loving me and keeping me free from condemnation.

In Jesus' Name, Amen.

For I know nothing against myself, yet I am not justified by this; but He who judges me is the Lord

1 Corinthians 4:4

Be encouraged, dear child of God, you can live completely free from condemnation and hold nothing against yourself because Jesus has fully cleared your record.

The only remedy for condemnation is the price Jesus paid.

Jesus is the way out of darkness because He is the way into the light of God's presence, where He ever-lives to makes intercession for you.

So don't hesitate, come to Jesus, He understands your pain because He suffered temptation just like you, yet without sinning.

You can trust Him to be very tender and merciful because He understands what you are going through. His grace is so powerful that no matter how deep the feelings of your pain He will set you free so you will never need to feel the pain of shame, guilt or condemnation again.

You may ask, is this possible on earth? I thought such freedom was only possible in heaven.

Oh no, dear child of God, this is exactly why Jesus paid such a high price for you in shedding His own precious blood. And this is why He is in heaven at the throne of God, so that through the work of His grace He can uphold you with His own righteousness and empower you to live the Life He has with the Father.

You may say, yes, this is wonderful, but what about those areas of my life where I still experience failure? Jesus will perfect that in you also as you abide in Him.

Now have a good look in the mirror of God's Word and you will no longer see yourself as a failure, a fool, or a sinner. You will see yourself blessed with every blessing in Jesus and greatly loved by the Father.

Let's pray: Heavenly Father, I thank You that through the work of Your grace I know nothing against myself. I believe You are upholding me with Your own righteousness and will perfect that which concerns me.

In Jesus' Name, Amen.

Whoever abides in Him does not sin. Whoever sins has neither seen Him nor knows Him

1 John 3:6

Jesus said, 'You will know that I am in My Father and that you are in Me, just as I am in you' (John 14:20 GNB).

The first thought Jesus gives is that you will know He is in the Father. In other words, you will come to know God as Father when you know Jesus. The second thought is just as amazing, that you will know Christ in you and you in Him.

This is more real than you may realise, for there is no real Christian Life outside of Jesus. This is why Jesus says when you abide in Him you will not sin because if you keep on sinning it shows you don't really know Him (1 John 3:5-6).

Now when you look into the mirror of His Word do you see yourself in Christ Jesus, thinking and acting like Him? Come, look more deeply into the perfect law of His Life. Can you see Christ in you, or do you not know you are a new creation, born of God? Do you not recognise His Life in you? Come and examine yourself as to whether you are truly in the faith. Test yourself. Do you not know that Jesus Christ is in you? (2 Corinthians 13:5).

This is why Jesus told you to abide in Him, and He in you, for without Him you can do nothing.

Even with the best intention never to sin (which is good, by the way) there is a law of sin and death in you from which you cannot escape without Jesus. That is why you must abide in Him, and He in you, for He is the only one able to keep you from sinning through His Life in you. His sinless Life in you is your freedom from sin!

You see through His death, Jesus shattered the power of your old sin-loving nature. When God with glorious power raised Jesus from the dead it was obvious sin had no dominion over Him. Now you are given His wonderful sinless Life to live.

So you can see that when you came to Christ (or, better still, when Christ came to live in you) your old sin-loving nature lost its power over you, for His sinless nature came to live in you. You are now free from sin through Jesus Christ to live to the glory of God!

The more you recognise the Life Jesus has with the Father in you, the more you will see yourself thinking, talking and acting like Him.

Let's pray: Heavenly Father, I know the Life You have given to Jesus in heaven is now in me for I am starting to think, talk and act like Him, free from sin. I love You Father.

In Jesus' Name, Amen.

For whoever calls on the name of the Lord shall be saved
Romans 10:13

The more the Holy Spirit reveals the Life Jesus has with the Father in you, the more you discover the unsearchable riches and glory of His grace.

Jesus Himself became the purchase price for your salvation!

This is why anyone who calls on the name of the Lord Jesus shall be saved!

What does it mean to be saved?

To be saved is to be whole, healed, secure, rescued from danger. Salvation means deliverance, preservation, prosperity, happiness, general well-being.

To be saved means no longer living for yourself, but surrendering your all to live for Him who loves you.

How great is the salvation that Jesus has won for us!

His salvation is nothing less than the greatness of the Life He has with the Father.

Dear child of God, if you still struggle with sin, do not be afraid, for the Lord Jesus is your salvation. There is no sin too strong for the Lord. He can utterly free you from everything that binds you. Remember Jesus defeated sin in His own body on the cross to forever free you from its power. Don't point your finger at anyone else, take responsibility for your own thoughts, words and actions, and come humbly before His throne of grace where you will find His mercy and grace to live the Life He has with the Father.

This was King David's prayer when he was overcoming sin in his own heart, 'Create in me a clean heart, O God, and renew a steadfast spirit within me. Restore to me the joy of Your salvation, and uphold me by Your generous Spirit' (Psalm 51:10,12).

Now you can pray, believing with all your heart that God raised Jesus from the dead and confessing with your mouth that He is Lord, so that you too will be saved (Romans 10:9)!

Let's pray: Heavenly Father, I humbly bow my knee and surrender my all to You. I do this because of Your grace, Your love, so richly given by Jesus Christ, my Lord and my Saviour. Thank You for saving me!

In Jesus' Name, Amen.

But when the kindness and the love of God our Saviour toward man appeared

Titus 3:4

The struggle for the soul that sinned to find God and escape the pain of failure can be unbearable. Oh the depth of darkness man can sink to when lost to God's love! What bitter evils can possess the soul of those who are separated from God!

But just as a bolt of lightning lights up the darkest sky, so Jesus comes for those in darkness.

What a wonderful Saviour we have in Jesus, who in His kindness and love is always ready to forgive every sin and cleanse us from all unrighteousness!

Has your heart ever cried out in utter desperation, 'Be merciful to me O God a sinner'?

Never forget, the loving-kindness of God our Saviour endures forever.

For John Newton, who wrote 'Amazing grace, how sweet the sound that saved a wretch like me,' this hymn was not just a beautiful poem, but a constant reminder that Jesus saved him from being an evil, murderous captain of a slave ship.

What kindness, what love divine, had saved him from such evil!

How can those who have sunk so deep in the mire of sinfulness be able to write such lasting songs of redemption? The answer is because Jesus is the same yesterday, today and forever (Hebrews 13:8)!

The same kindness and love that saved John Newton is now moving throughout the entire world to seek and save the lost.

This kindness becomes even more glorious when you consider that William Wilberforce went to John Newton for prayer and inspiration to abolish the slave trade – the very trade that Newton had once promoted!

Rather than limiting the Almighty, I pray your heart - like that of John Newton - will always sing of God's 'Amazing Grace' so that your life will be an inspiration for others to find the loving-kindness Jesus gives from His Life with the Father.

Let's pray: Heavenly Father, open my eyes to Your love and kindness and let it flow through me like a river because Your loving-kindness is better than life, my lips shall praise You. Thus I will bless You while I live; I will lift up my hands in Your name.

In Jesus' Name, Amen.

Amazing Grace, how sweet the sound,
That saved a wretch like me.
I once was lost but now am found,
Was blind, but now I see.

T'was Grace that taught my heart to fear.
And Grace, my fears relieved.
How precious did that Grace appear
The hour I first believed.

Through many dangers, toils and snares
I have already come;
'Tis Grace that brought me safe thus far
and Grace will lead me home.

The Lord has promised good to me.
His word my hope secures.
He will my shield and portion be,
As long as life endures.

Yea, when this flesh and heart shall fail,
And mortal life shall cease,
I shall possess within the veil,
A life of joy and peace.

When we've been here ten thousand years
Bright shining as the sun.
We've no less days to sing God's praise
Than when we've first begun.

John Newton, 1779.

Not by works of righteousness which we have done, but according to His mercy He saved us, through the washing of regeneration and renewing of the Holy Spirit

Titus 3:5

Let this truth deeply penetrate your heart - that it is not because of any good deed you have done, but because of God's mercy, that you are saved.

What is God's mercy? It is most wonderful. It means His loving-kindness, His unfailing love for you, His tenderness. Above all else it means His faithfulness.

You see God's mercy is deeper than the deepest ocean and higher than the highest heavens. His compassion for lost sinners is not just some sense of pity, but an active work of His self-sacrificing love which He manifested in Jesus on the cross.

When Jesus took the whole weight of the law in Himself – the law that we failed to obey - He nailed it to the cross and thereby demonstrated God's mercy which triumphs over judgment. When you think of God's mercy, think of Jesus pleading for sinners as He shed His blood to ransom you from the judgment of God's wrath. It is thanks to the blood of Jesus that you are saved by His mercy instead of having to suffer His judgment. It is because of His mercy that you can receive forgiveness, righteousness, peace and joy instead of condemnation.

God's mercy goes way beyond the simple act of giving you a second chance. He gives you a whole new nature through the washing of regeneration and by the renewing of the Holy Spirit, transforming and enriching your whole life.

When you are being washed by the Holy Spirit you are not just freed from feelings that are wrong, selfish, hateful, angry, envious, bitter, jealous, lustful, unloving, unholy and ungodly, but you are given feelings of God's wonderful love, peace, joy, longsuffering, kindness, goodness, faithfulness, gentleness and self-control. These heavenly graces begin to empower you to love others as God loves you.

It is so beautiful to see a soul saved; it makes angels rejoice.

What mighty things God can do through you when you have received His mercy.

Let's pray: Heavenly Father, if it was not for Your mercy I would have been lost forever. Your mercies are new every morning; great is Your faithfulness, Your love and kindness to me.

In Jesus' Name, Amen.

For if when we were enemies we were reconciled to God through the death of His Son, much more, having been reconciled, we shall be saved by His life

Romans 5:10

Will God show more love for sinners than for His own children? Will He forgive a sinner more readily than you? Of course not!

When you were without Jesus you thought like a sinner and prayed like a sinner, begging God for mercy because you felt separated from Him as you had no defense against sin. Now that you are His child, you pray completely differently. Sure, you may weep when you feel the pain of sin and suffer the abuse of Satan's accusations, but you no longer pray like a stranger but like a child of God: 'Our Father who is in heaven, forgive me my trespasses as I also forgive those who trespass against me' (Matthew 6:12). Now you know that if you confess your sins, He is faithful and just to forgive you and cleanse you from all unrighteousness (1 John 1:9). And you also know you can come boldly to His throne of grace and find the merciful Jesus to help you in your time of need (Hebrews 4:16). Now you know His Spirit will not only wash you with His blood but teach you to abide in Him.

Therefore you no longer place your hope in your own best efforts but trust in Jesus to keep you through the Life He has with the Father. For you know that as you abide in Him who cannot sin, nor will you.

Oh, the blessings that God gives you through Jesus are so wonderful!

He gives you so much more now you are His child; He gives you His Life, a Life that knows no sin.

Come dear child of God, let your faith rise and triumph over all sin through Jesus Christ. He will never fail you. Begin to praise Him for all He has done for you!

Jesus is upholding you with His own righteousness. He lives in you with the Life He has with the Father. Trust in Jesus for His love for you will never fail. Only believe!

Let's pray: Heavenly Father, I know You love me and keep me free from sin through the power of Jesus Christ in me. Thank You for forgiving me so graciously and granting me the privilege of sharing the Life Jesus has with You.

In Jesus' Name, Amen.

And from Jesus Christ, the faithful witness, the firstborn from the dead, and the ruler over the kings of the earth. To Him who loved us and washed us from our sins in His own blood

Revelations 1:5

Who in heaven and earth or in all creation can withstand Jesus, who gave His precious blood to wash away the deepest stain of our sins? To Him belong the kingdom and the power and the glory forever and ever, Amen.

Consider, dear child of God, the greatness of the power of Jesus' blood – 'When a great multitude which no one can number, of all nations, tribes, peoples, and tongues, is standing before the throne of God and before the Lamb clothed with white robes, with palm branches in their hands, crying out with a loud voice, saying, 'Salvation belongs to our God who sits on the throne, and to the Lamb!' These are the ones who have washed their robes and made them white in the blood of the Lamb. Therefore they are before the throne of God, and serve Him day and night. And He who sits on the throne will dwell among them, for the Lamb who is in the midst of the throne will shepherd them and lead them to living fountains of waters. And God will wipe away every tear from their eyes' (Revelation 7).

You see Jesus has all the power in His blood to make you clean, holy and without blame. 'Come, let's talk this over!' says the Lord, 'no matter how deep the stain of your sins, I can take it out and make you as clean as freshly fallen snow. Even if you are stained as red as crimson, I can make you white as wool! If you will only let me help you, if you will only obey, then I will make you rich!' (Isaiah 1:18-20 LB). You no longer have to live with the effects of past sins, for Jesus has the power through His blood to make all things new, to wash you white as snow.

This is one of the foremost ministries of the Holy Spirit in you - to wash you with the blood of Jesus and take away all consciousness of sin. What indescribable joy for your whole spirit, soul and body to be holy, filled with the riches of the righteousness, peace and joy Jesus enjoys in the presence of the Father.

This is the will of the Father, that you live in such a place of His grace and favour that no one would dare bring a charge against you (Romans 8:31-35). Now lift your hands in praise for the glory of God's grace. To Him who loved us and washed us from our sins in His own blood, and has made us kings and priests to His God and Father, to Him be glory and dominion forever and ever. Amen.

Let's pray: Heavenly Father, You gave Jesus the kingdom, the power and the glory for He is the Lamb of God who takes away the sin of the world. He has washed me in His own precious blood to bring me to You. I worship You.

In Jesus' name, Amen.

*For he who lacks these things is short-sighted, even to blindness,
and has forgotten that he was cleansed from his old sins*

2 Peter 1:9

Is it possible for those who have lived in freedom and tasted the
good Life, to come to slip back into the old nature of sin, into the
love of the world and its deceiving pleasures?

Could someone be so deceived and blinded that they would no
longer rejoice in Jesus and live the Life He has with the Father?

You know you were recreated through His Life in you to live
forever in His presence. However, the stark reality of sin is that it
can cause your soul to suffer the unimaginable sorrows of hell.
Heaven and hell are real places!

The only security you have that you will not go to hell but go to
heaven, is the Life of Jesus in you (1 John 5:12). This is why He
is at the throne of God, so that He can assure your heart before
Him that you have eternal Life.

You know His Life and ministry at the Father's right hand is to
secure your eternal salvation. Jesus said, 'I will go and prepare a
place for you so that where I am you may be also' (John 14:2).
Therefore your hope can be in nothing less than Jesus Christ and
His righteousness!

No self-effort can secure such absolute, complete, unshakable and
everlasting salvation. Only the Life of Jesus can do this. Nor is
there salvation in any other, for there is no other name under
heaven given among men by which we must be saved (Acts 4:12).
Jesus alone can keep you from stumbling through the Life He has
with the Father and present you faultless before the presence of
His glory with exceeding joy (Jude 24).

Trust in Jesus, for it is by hearing the good news of what He has done for you that you were marked as belonging to Him by the Holy Spirit. And the Holy Spirit's presence within you is God's guarantee that He has purchased you and guarantees to bring you to Himself. So don't be afraid, dear child of God, only believe; Jesus will never leave you and the Holy Spirit whom He has given you will be with you and in you forever (Matthew 28:20; John 14:16).

Let's pray: Heavenly Father, I know You love me. I know Jesus ever lives to make intercession for me so that I may live the Life He has with You. I love You Father and trust You to keep me.

In Jesus' Name, Amen.

Now the just shall live by faith. But if anyone draws back, my soul has no pleasure in him

Hebrews 10:38

It is beautiful to see a trusting heart that has no guile but is completely at rest. Such a heart of faith commands great power - Jesus said that all things are possible to him who believes.

This is what God is looking for, those who trust Him! The eyes of the Lord are intently watching those who have placed their trust in Him; He hears their cry when they call on Him and they are given every blessing, including His wonderful peace. He personally takes care of them when the road is rough and rescues them when they slip or fall. The Lord has never forsaken the person who trusts in Him; they patiently wait for Him to act and always end up with the most remarkable stories of the miracles of His grace (Psalm 37 LB).

Abraham was such a man. When he shared his great pain with God - that He had not given him any children, since his wife was barren - God said, 'Don't be afraid about your future; I am your protection and the guarantee of every blessing.' God showed Abraham the stars of heaven and the sand by the sea and said, 'So shall your seed be,' and Abraham believed God and it was credited to him as righteousness (Genesis 15).

Through faith Abraham developed a beautiful friendship with God. Even though it seemed impossible, Abraham had such hope through faith that he did not give way to feelings of despair, but rather praised God that what He promised He would do.

Oh, how it pleased God that Abraham never looked at what he could not do, but always looked to what God could do. God gave Abraham what He promised, as he became the father of many nations.

Those who are made right in God's sight are truly living by faith.

Be encouraged, dear child of God, all the rich and wonderful blessings of the Life Jesus has with the Father are yours.

If you feel powerless and everything seems impossible, follow Abraham's example; stay in faith, receive God's Life, and give Him the praise.

Let's pray: Heavenly Father, I know all Your promises are true; this is why I look to You. Purify and perfect my heart to always love and trust You.

In Jesus' Name, Amen.

And the peace of God, which surpasses all understanding, will guard your hearts and minds through Christ Jesus
Philippians 4:7

The great gift of God in salvation is a new heart with right desires - a heart that always wants what He wants and a new mind that knows what He wants.

Jesus said that a good man brings forth good from the treasure of his heart. In other words, the quality of life is determined by what comes from the heart.

Think about the young man Jesus told about in Luke 15. He left his father's house and had all to live for but wasted what was given on prodigal living. When he began to be in want he came to himself.

You see this is a gift of God, granting your heart to realise the good things that await you in His presence. The young man returned to his father with a humble heart. Oh, the joy of the Father to see his lost son come home; he ran to him, embraced him, forgave him, restored him and blessed him.

Now this is the peace of God, it is not just a feeling; the peace, prosperity and wholeness that awaits you in God's presence is no less than the Life Jesus has with the Father.

Peace is therefore not just the absence of problems, it is much better than that; it is the joy of the love and kindness of the Father. With this joy in your heart you can face anything and know all is well. This is why God's Word says to you, 'Don't worry about anything; instead, pray about everything; tell God your needs and don't forget to thank Him for His answers. If you do this you will experience God's peace, which is far more wonderful than the human mind can understand. His peace will keep your thoughts and your hearts quiet and at rest as you trust in Christ Jesus.' (Philippians 4:6-7 LB).

Let the peace of God flood every part of your heart and mind today.

Let's pray: Heavenly Father, Your Life is better, Your love is greater, than anything else. You give me so much more than I have ever had before. Thank You for keeping my heart and mind in Your perfect peace.

In Jesus' Name, Amen.

We love Him because He first loved us

1 John 4:19

It is only when Jesus takes away your sins that you truly discover how much God loves you.

When the Holy Spirit pours God's love into your heart, then you begin to see that God is love and you are greatly loved by Him. Then you will realise that your worth is more than all the wealth on earth.

Oh dear child of God, can't you see how precious you are? Think about this: The Father demonstrated His love for you so much that while yet a sinner, Jesus died for you, so that now through His Life you may live the Life He has with the Father.

This is love, not that you loved God, but that He first loved you!

You may weep under the strain of your human nature and say, 'But how long, Heavenly Father, must I persevere in faith towards what you called me to in Jesus? When will I see your glory? When will I be transformed from glory unto glory?'

Be greatly encouraged and take comfort; weeping may endure for the night but joy comes in the morning (Psalm 30:5).

Fix your eyes on the joy set before you, when one day you will see Jesus, and then, in the twinkling of an eye, you will be made glorious in His likeness when He presents you to the Father, perfect and well pleasing in His sight.

There will be no time for weeping then when your mouth is filled with laughter and your tongue with singing as you stand before His throne of grace and praise Him, saying, 'Worthy is the Lamb who was slain! Blessing and honour and glory and power belong to Him who sits on the throne, and to the Lamb, forever and ever!' (Revelation 5:12, 13).

Now take great comfort, for the Holy Spirit is here to give you a foretaste of your Life in glory and open your understanding to the joy set before you, even while you are persevering in the time you have on earth.

Let's pray: Heavenly Father, how great Thou art! Then sings my soul, my Saviour God, to Thee! How great Thou art that You loved me first. I love You Heavenly Father!

In Jesus' Name, Amen.

O Lord my God! When I in awesome wonder
Consider all the works Thy hand hath made,
I see the stars, I hear the mighty thunder,
Thy power throughout the universe displayed;

Refrain:
Then sings my soul, my Saviour God, to Thee,
How great Thou art, how great Thou art!
Then sings my soul, my Saviour God, to Thee,
How great Thou art, how great Thou art!

When through the woods and forest glades I wander
and hear the birds sing sweetly in the trees;
when I look down from lofty mountain grandeur,
and hear the brook, and feel the gentle breeze;

And when I think that God His Son not sparing,
Sent Him to die - I scarce can take it in,
That on the cross my burden gladly bearing,
He bled and died to take away my sin:

When Christ shall come with shout of acclamation
And take me home- what joy shall fill my heart!
Then I shall bow in humble adoration
And there proclaim, my God, how great Thou art!

Cark Gustav Boberg, 1885, and Stuart Hine, 1949.

LET IT BE TO ME ACCORDING
TO YOUR WORD

And He said to me, 'My grace is sufficient for you, for My strength is made perfect in weakness.' Therefore most gladly I will rather boast in my infirmities, that the power of Christ may rest upon me

2 Corinthians 12:9

When Jesus says, 'My grace is sufficient for you,' He is saying, 'No matter how weak you are, out of the abundance of the Life I have with the Father, I give you grace upon grace, blessings upon blessings, gifts heaped upon gifts' (John 1:16 AMPB).

You see, Jesus lifts you from the frailty of your human nature to embrace the riches of the glory He has with the Father. His word becomes alive in you, filling your heart with His faith - the gift of the Holy Spirit. Yes, every good gift from above is given to you until you become wholly filled and flooded with God Himself.

Remember when the Angel Gabriel said to Mary, 'Rejoice, highly favoured one, the Lord is with you; you are blessed for you have found favour with God'? The Holy Spirit came upon Mary and the power of the Most High overshadowed her so that Jesus the Son of God was born in her (Luke 1:28-38). The way Mary responded is what God is looking for in you. She said, 'Let it be to me according to Your word.'

Now let every fear and worry dissipate in the light of God's truth, for it will be done to you according to His word! Jesus the Son of God is born in you and every good and perfect gift of the Life He has with the Father is yours. Begin therefore to believe; pray and say, 'Thank You Father that in nothing I will fall short of Your glory.' This is what Jesus means when He says, 'My grace is sufficient for you!'

Remember when Jairus came to Jesus because his daughter was desperately ill? Jesus responded immediately. But while on the way, the report came that it was too late. But Jesus said, 'Don't be afraid; only believe!' All Jairus had to do was to believe the word of Jesus. This is God's grace for you. Your response must be, 'Only believe!'

Jesus took Jairus to a whole new height of His grace and blessings because even though his daughter had died, she came back to life. There is really nothing too difficult for the Lord Jesus as long as you keep trusting Him as Jairus did.

Let's pray: Heavenly Father, Your grace is sufficient for me. I believe that nothing is too difficult for You. I trust You; let it be done to me according to Your word.

In Jesus' Name, Amen.

Then he said to them, 'Go your way, eat the fat, drink the sweet, and send portions to those for whom nothing is prepared; for this day is holy to our Lord. Do not sorrow, for the joy of the Lord is your strength'

Nehemiah 8:10

You have heard it said, 'The joy of the Lord is your strength.' This is true. We all enjoy life more when we feel encouraged.

King David understood this principle, which is why he strengthened himself in the Lord (1 Samuel 30.6).

This is why God's Word for you today is: 'Cheer up, don't be afraid! For the Lord your God has arrived to live among you. He is a mighty Saviour. He will give you victory. He will rejoice over you in great gladness. He will love you and not accuse you. Is that a joyous choir I hear? No, it is the Lord Himself exulting over you in happy song' (Zephaniah 3.16-18 LB).

Thank God we have the written Word to remind us how to be strong in faith and very encouraged. This is how Jesus overcame those moments when Satan pushed Him to doubt the Father's love. He simply said, 'It is written, 'Man shall not live by bread alone, but by every word of God" (Luke 4:4).

Now you have the written Word of God to find strength and encouragement in the hour of your need. When God's Word lives in your heart, you have all the courage of faith you need to see the impossible become possible!

Before Joshua entered God's promised blessings, God said to him, 'Meditate in My Word day and night. Do not let it depart from your mouth for then you will make your way prosper and you will have good success. Have I not commanded you? Be strong and of good courage, do not be afraid, nor be dismayed, for the Lord is with you wherever you go' (Joshua 1:5-8).

When Joshua came to the end of his journey, he said, 'Not one thing has failed of all the good things which the Lord your God spoke concerning you. All have come to pass for you; not one word of them has failed' (Joshua 23:14b).

Always know and be confident of this: it makes the Father very happy to encourage you, blessing you with every blessing, for He loves to see you prosper in both body and soul (3 John 2).

So rejoice in the Lord, stand in His Word, and be strong and very encouraged.

Let's pray: Heavenly Father, Your word is in my heart, therefore I will say what You say and do what You do. I believe You rejoice to see me prosper in all things and be in health.

In Jesus' Name, Amen.

Then the angel said to her, 'Do not be afraid, Mary, for you have found favour with God'

Luke 1:30

Jesus told a most beautiful parable to describe the amazing blessing of finding favour with God.

A shepherd had one hundred sheep but left the ninety-nine to find one that was lost. When he found it, he had greater joy over the one he found than the ninety-nine who were safe (Luke 15).

Can you see how deeply concerned God is that you live in His care? He wants you to live the Life Jesus lives in His presence and enjoy all His wonderful blessings. He does not hide His favour from you, quite the opposite! His favour is seeking you.

There are many goals to pursue in life, but the most important of all is to live in God's favour.

King David said, 'O Lord God, why have You showered Your blessings on such an insignificant person as I am? Oh, Lord God! What can I say? For You know what I am like! You are doing all these things just because You promised to and because You want to! How great You are, Lord God!' (1 Samuel 7:18-21 LB).

Remember when David was young, he dared to face Goliath in the name of the Lord with a sling and a few stones and he was able to defeat that big giant because God favoured him.

When you live in God's favour you learn to say, 'I can do all things through Christ who strengthens me' (Philippians 4:13).

This is why the Bible says, 'They did not conquer by their own strength and skill, but by Your mighty power and because You smiled upon them and favoured them' (Psalm 44:3 LB).

Martin Luther, who faced immense challenges and pressures but was able to bring great blessing to others, once said this: 'I have such a busy day tomorrow, I shall spend the first three hours in prayer lest Satan get the best of me.'

Everyone who has tasted and seen that the Lord is good knows their success is because of God's favour. There is no greater favour than to live the Life Jesus has with the Father and be blessed with the riches of His glory!

Let's pray: Heavenly Father, I was lost but You found me, I was blind but now I see You care for me. I love You Father; You are so good to me!

In Jesus' Name, Amen.

And do not be conformed to this world, but be transformed by the renewing of your mind, that you may prove what is that good and acceptable and perfect will of God

Romans 12:2

Sometimes we look for circumstances to change without realising that change starts in the way we think.

Smith Wigglesworth tells a wonderful story of how his sister Mary came to see a big steel locomotive and said to him, 'It will never go!' But Smith kept encouraging her to trust him and get in. When she finally did, he pulled a few levers and blew the whistle and it went. When that heavy railway train started moving Mary shouted, 'It will never stop! It will never stop!'

This is what some think about the Life of Jesus: It is not for me; I have made too many mistakes; I am too weak.

Is it possible you can be so set in your ways that you limit God? When God brought the prophet Ezekiel into a valley full of dry dead bones, He asked him, 'Can these bones live?' Now anyone would think that a strange question. Of course they can never live again. But not this man, he kept his mind open to the thoughts of God and said, 'O Lord God, You know.'

Then God said to him, 'Speak to these bones', and when he did, suddenly there came a great sound as the bones came together and sinews and flesh came upon them and they became a great army. This was God's way of showing the prophet what He could do to restore a hopeless people (Ezekiel 37).

What a glorious transformation God has for those who let Him renew their mind.

You see God desires to open your understanding to the Life Jesus has with Him so He can transform and renew you to live like Him.

Don't limit God by limiting yourself!

Even as a newborn child learns how to speak by daily hearing new sounds, so you need to let God's Word fill your heart so you can learn to think, talk and act like Him.

So let His limitless Life transform your limited thinking today!

Let's pray: Heavenly Father, I desire to be of one heart and mind with You, to think like You and live the Life You give me in an unlimited way.

In Jesus' Name, Amen.

If you do well, will you not be accepted? And if you do not do well, sin lies at the door. And its desire is for you, but you should rule over it

Genesis 4:7

There are many things that come knocking on the door of your heart, but it is up to you which thoughts you entertain. Learn to keep your heart with all diligence, for out of it spring the issues of life (Proverbs 4:23).

In Genesis chapter 4, we see how God came to Cain who was having evil thoughts, and told him to rule over them.

We need to learn to rule over wrong thoughts and take them captive and not speak them out or act on them. When we cast down an evil imagination and choose to think the thoughts of God we will see His blessings overtake us.

Much of the way we live is determined by the way we think. We must never let Satan get a grip on us, like he did on Cain, by twisting our thoughts!

Thought patterns can so easily become strongholds – a stronghold over the way we look at things. There are godly strongholds of love and faith and there are ungodly strongholds of fear and evil. These thought patterns are developed over time and determine how we act or react.

To break wrong thought patterns is what the Bible calls being renewed in your mind. This is one of the great gifts Jesus gives through His Life in you. You see Jesus will write His Word in your heart so you will want what He wants, and He will write His Word in your mind so you will know what He wants.

I learned an important lesson when I was young. My father had given my brother a digital watch which I could not take my eyes off. Then my father came home with a new red box and said to me, 'You can have what is in this box or you can have your brother's watch.' Without thinking I took my brother's watch and walked off laughing, until I found out what was in the box - it was exactly the colour and kind of watch I wanted.

I am happy I learned my lesson while I was young – and that only with a watch! I learned to rejoice with others in how God blessed them and trust that He has what is best for me.

Let's pray: Heavenly Father, I thank You for helping me to think like You because I know what You have is the best for me.
In Jesus' Name, Amen.

To the pure all things are pure, but to those who are defiled and unbelieving nothing is pure; but even their mind and conscience are defiled

Titus 1:15

One lady asked her husband how the neighbours across the street could hang out such dirty clothes to dry. Did they not know how to wash? Every day she saw those clothes she became more frustrated, until one day she looked out of the window and they were all perfectly clean. She said to her husband, 'Look! They finally got their clothes clean.' With a smile her husband said, 'I cleaned our windows this morning.'

It is amazing how we can see things from our own perspective and not realise that it is perhaps we who need our windows washed.

The Bible talks about not leaning on your own understanding or being wise in your own eyes but trusting in the Lord with all your heart (Proverbs 3.5-8).

While King David was a man after God's own heart, there were times in his life that even he needed his own windows washed. David prayed earnestly, 'Create in me a clean heart, O God, and renew a steadfast spirit within me' (Psalm 51.10).

Always remember that it is the Father's great pleasure - because of what Jesus has done for you - to give you the Holy Spirit, who will continually cleanse you so you can clearly see, hear and perceive things from a pure heart and mind.

You see the Father wants you to know Him and Jesus Christ whom He sent (John 17:3). This is why most of all He will create a pure heart and mind in you, so you may know the ever-living hope of the Life He has called you to in Jesus and the unsearchable riches of this Life already working in you through the same power by which He raised Jesus from the dead and seated Him at His right hand (Ephesians 1:17-20).

Because of this take a moment and lift your hands in praise to the Father for giving you the Holy Spirit who is purifying your heart through faith in Jesus. And let the roots of your faith grow deep into Jesus Himself, as you trust Him to fill you with the Life He has with the Father.

Let's pray: Heavenly Father, create a pure heart and mind in me so I may know the Life Jesus has with You in me.

In Jesus' Name, Amen.

And you shall know the truth, and the truth shall make you free
John 8:32

It is wonderful when the light of the Life that God has given Jesus at His throne begins to shine in your heart and you discover the truth and freedom Jesus gives.

Be encouraged, for the Lord is good and He is glad to show you the proper path. He will teach you the ways that are right and best when you humbly turn to Him. And when you obey Him, every path He guides you on is fragrant with His loving kindness and truth.

Where is the man who fears the Lord? God will teach him how to choose the best. He shall live within God's circle of blessing (Psalm 25:8-10, 12-13 LB).

The truth empowers you to choose life or death. This was certainly true for Adam and Eve. God told Adam he could freely eat of every tree, but would die the day he ate of the tree of the knowledge of good and evil. Adam had the power to choose life or death. What you want to know always reveals your real character.

Jesus said, 'This is eternal life, that they may know You, the only true God, and Jesus Christ whom You have sent' (John 17:3).

This is the truth of the Life in you, that you know, recognise and perceive the Father and the Son inwardly.

You see the Father has commanded the light of His Life to shine in your heart to give you knowledge and understanding of the truth that the Life Jesus has with the Father is now in you.

The more you recognise the Father and the Son through His Life in you, the more you will experience God's grace and peace.

So you see you can now enjoy living a truly godly life (2 Peter 1:2-8).

Let's pray: Heavenly Father, how I love the light of Your Life in me! I know the truth that this Life comes from You.

In Jesus' Name, Amen.

So he, trembling and astonished, said, 'Lord, what do You want me to do?' Then the Lord said to him, 'Arise and go into the city, and you will be told what you must do'

Acts 9:6

When Saul met Jesus, he was on his way to do all he could against Him. On the Damascus Road, Jesus appeared and said to Saul, 'I am Jesus!' This revelation of Jesus transformed Saul to Paul. The persecutor became the preacher as the old life died when the new Life of Jesus came into his heart.

When Jesus is revealed in you, you are born again; you instantly become a new creation, a member of God's household and an heir of the Life Jesus has with the Father.

You see Jesus is your Life, and God in His perfect love for you has seen to it that this Life that now lives in you by the Holy Spirit is kept perfectly safe in the body of Jesus at His right hand, so that nothing will ever be able to separate you from His love.

I pray this revelation fills your heart as it helps you through the struggles that come by living in a human body on earth.

Be encouraged dear child of God, you will find rest in Jesus for He is able to maintain His Life in you, so that like the Apostle Paul, you will see that your old sin-loving nature was crucified with Him, and that the Life you now live is the Life of Jesus who loves you and gave Himself for you. This revelation of Christ in you helps you discover what He wants you to do because Jesus wants you to live through Him to tell the world about Him.

When Paul met Jesus and asked Him, 'What do You want me to do?' Jesus said, 'Rise and stand on your feet; for I have appeared to you for this purpose, to make you a minister and a witness both of the things which you have seen and the things which I will yet reveal to you' (Acts 26:16).

Now that Paul is in heaven, it is your turn to rise in the revelation of Jesus in you and tell others about Him.

If you feel ill-equipped for this privilege, lift up your eyes for it pleases the Father to reveal His Son in you to empower you (Galatians 1:15-16).

Let's pray: Heavenly Father, thank You for revealing Your Son in me. You have given me new Life in Him and I trust You to keep revealing Jesus in me so that I may have the power to tell others about Him.

In Jesus' Name, Amen.

This is a faithful saying and worthy of all acceptance, that Christ
Jesus came into the world to save sinners, of whom I am chief
1 Timothy 1:15

Paul believed his salvation was not just for himself, but to give
hope to anyone who would believe in Jesus. You see through the
Life and love of Jesus in you, you will know God desires all men
to be saved (1 Timothy 2:4).

People would hear about the powerful things God worked
through Paul, read his letters and think he must be some amazing
man; but when they met him in person they were surprised
because he was like any other man. Paul said, 'I know you think
I am but a mere human and of course I am. But what I do, I do
not do by my own ability but by God's mighty power working
through me' (2 Corinthians 10).

This is why Paul talked about his salvation experience, to
demonstrate the power of Jesus to save to the uttermost. When
Jesus appeared to him He made Paul a minister and witness (Acts
26:16). This is why Paul said, 'You can see that the gospel I preach
is not a human invention but came through the revelation of
Jesus' (Galatians 1:11-12). Every time Paul talked about Jesus,
God anointed him with the Holy Spirit to convince those who
heard him about the truth of Jesus. As Paul spoke, the Spirit of
God began to open their eyes in order to turn them from darkness
to light, and from the power of Satan to God, that they may
receive forgiveness of sins and an inheritance among those who
are sanctified by faith in Jesus (Acts 26:18).

Paul had discovered the good news about Jesus is the power of
God unto salvation for everyone who believes, for in it is revealed
the righteousness of God through faith in Jesus. But how can

anyone believe in Jesus if they have never heard about Him? How can anyone tell others about Jesus and help them to experience His saving power if they don't know Him themselves?

But you do know Him for He lives in you by the Holy Spirit, and therefore you can expect that every time you talk about Jesus, God will anoint you to convince those who hear you to believe in Jesus and be saved.

Let's pray: Heavenly Father, I thank You that every time I talk about Jesus, You will anoint me with the Holy Spirit so all who hear me will believe in Jesus and be saved.

In Jesus' Name, Amen.

Then he said to Jesus, 'Lord, remember me when You come into Your kingdom'

Luke 23:42

Luke's Gospel tells us that there was a man hanging on a cross next to Jesus who heard Him pray, 'Father, forgive them for they know not what they do.' He also heard the voice of another crucified man on the other side of Jesus shouting with bitter anger, 'If You are the Christ, save Yourself and us.'

Now the first man could do one of three things: Do nothing and die in sorrow; join the angry man in scorning Jesus; or, listen to Jesus and find salvation.

He chose to listen to Jesus.

He rebuked the angry man saying, 'Do you not even fear God, seeing you are under the same condemnation? And we indeed justly, for we receive the due reward of our deeds; but this man has done nothing wrong.' Then he said to Jesus, 'Lord, remember me when You come into Your kingdom.' And Jesus said to him, 'Assuredly, I say to you, today you will be with me in paradise' (Luke 23:39-43).

The truth is that we all have a choice. We can join those who scorn or those who reach out to Jesus.

Sometimes in life you can feel there is no way back; but that is not true. The Psalmist said, 'When I thought about the wrong direction in which I was headed, and turned around, I came running back to You' (Psalm 119:59-60 LB).

Both these men who were crucified next to Jesus heard Him pray, 'Father, forgive them.'

The one who humbly sought forgiveness found salvation and oh what glory filled his soul.

Whenever you humbly turn from evil and come to Jesus with a broken and a contrite heart you will always find His mercy ready to forgive and receive the wonderful life He gives.

Let's pray: Heavenly Father, You are so good to me; Your mercies are new every morning. I love You and thank You for loving me.
In Jesus' Name, Amen.

Do you not know that the unrighteous will not inherit the kingdom of God? Do not to be deceived, neither fornicators, nor idolaters, nor adulterers, nor homosexuals, nor covetous, nor drunkards, nor revilers, nor extortioners will inherit the kingdom of God. And such were some of you. But you were washed, but you were sanctified, but you were justified in the name of the Lord Jesus and by the Spirit of our God

1 Corinthians 6:9-11

Dear child of God, it is important to know that there are lifestyles in this world that are contrary to God's will and nature. The above list is by no means inclusive of all sin, but it does remind you that Jesus came to wash away these deceptions. Jesus often warned of the terrible consequences of unrepentant sins that separate someone from God and can cause them to go to hell - a place of fire and unimaginable suffering (Luke 16:19-31).

I hear the hymn within my heart as I write this: 'Then sings my soul, my Saviour God to Thee, how great Thou art, how great Thou art!'

You see, sin had left a terrible stain upon your soul so that you could not see who God planned you to be. But no matter how deep the stain of sin, Jesus paid the price in full in order to wash you white as snow.

What an overwhelming joy to be washed and made whole by the Lord Jesus and the Spirit of God so that you can reflect His image every time you look into the mirror of His Word and see yourself holy and well pleasing in His sight.

I pray that you may shout to God with a voice of triumph, that the deception of sin is broken!

Jesus set you free!

His Life in you shows you are free - free indeed!

Now breathe the fresh air of the love of Jesus for you are free from condemnation to enjoy all the rich blessings of His Life in you.

Let's pray: Heavenly Father, there are no words to describe how grateful I am to be washed and made pure and clean by the Lord Jesus and Your Spirit so I can always see You in me and reflect Your image.

In Jesus' Name, Amen.

Peace I leave with you, My peace I give to you; not as the world gives do I give to you. Let not your heart be troubled, neither let it be afraid

John 14:27

When Jesus talks about giving you His peace, He is talking about the peace He enjoys at the throne of God, where He reigns victorious. This peace far surpasses our understanding because it is not of this world. It is a peace which has a heavenly capacity to guard your heart and mind no matter what you're going through. Even in the roughest storms of life, when all else seems to fail, you will have His peace to stay calm and see everything turn for good.

When the late mother Teresa of Calcutta was given the Nobel peace prize, she was asked by world leaders, 'What must we do to bring peace to the world?' She answered, 'Go home and love your family!' When you feel compelled to do great things for the good of man, remember this starts at home, in your own heart and family.

How we live every day, both in private and public, matters!

Jesus is the Saviour of the world because He lived in unbroken fellowship with the Father and was enabled by Him to carry the weight of the world on His shoulders.

While it was glorious to be anointed with the Holy Spirit and power and to go about doing good, healing all who were oppressed by the devil, all this was not without nights of prayer and many tears.

You see the Life Jesus has with the Father which is now revealed in you, is not just for yourself but is to share with everyone else. In the process of sharing His wonderful Life, you will at times feel what others feel and suffer their pain. But whenever you do this in prayer, praise and tears before God, you will see the great resources of His peace begin to flow through you like a river.

I pray your life becomes a great channel of the peace Jesus has with the Father!

Jesus said, 'Blessed are the peacemakers, for they shall be called sons of God' (Matthew 5:9).

Let's pray: Heavenly Father, I trust You to keep my heart and mind in perfect peace and make me a channel of Your peace.

In Jesus' Name, Amen.

Of the increase of His government and peace there will be no end, upon the throne of David and over His kingdom, to order it and establish it with judgment and justice from this time forward, even forever. The zeal of the Lord of host will perform this

Isaiah 9:7

It is important we are regularly reminded that Jesus has all authority and power in heaven and earth. He is on the throne and He reigns. This is what amazed the disciples, when they saw everything made subject to Him. The waves of the sea and the wind obeyed Him; demons were afraid of Him; death fled before Him and sickness bowed the knee to Him. After all the great works Jesus showed from the Father, He said 'You will see greater works for I go to the Father' (John 14:12).

Come, dear child of God, let the all-powerful Saviour of your soul, Jesus, lift you into the Life He has with the Father. There is no sorrow or situation too great or small for Him.

Jesus is called Wonderful, Counsellor, Mighty God, Everlasting Father, and Prince of Peace (Isaiah 9:6). He is all-powerful, all-sufficient and eternally capable of being all you need for perfect peace, wholeness and wellbeing.

This all-sufficiency of God's nature is seen throughout Scripture as He reveals Himself.

Abraham saw this when he was a hundred years old and his wife Sarah ninety-one, when God enabled her to conceive and bring forth a son, Isaac.

Moses brought Israel out of bondage through the terrible wilderness and Joshua led them triumphantly to possess the Promised Land.

These were great events that stand out to encourage our faith, but they by no means overshadow the smallest miracles of God's grace.

Be encouraged dear child of God, even if you feel powerless and weak, Jesus is on the throne. Your weakness does not hinder His all-sufficient grace. You will see His strength revealed in you even more than before.

When Jethro, the father-in-law of Moses, heard of all the Lord had done he said, 'Now I know that the Lord is greater than all the gods; for in the very thing in which they behaved proudly, He was above them' (Exodus 18:11).

Jesus is the Name above every other name! Jesus is Lord!

Let's pray: Heavenly Father, You have given all authority and power in heaven and earth to Jesus my Lord. I trust You are in control of my life and will work all things together for my good.

In Jesus' Name, Amen.

The work of righteousness will be peace and the effect of righteousness, quietness and assurance forever
                                              Isaiah 32:17

Perfect peace always follows perfect righteousness, and perfect righteousness is a gift of God to all who believe in Jesus. For God was in Christ reconciling the world to Himself, by not imputing our trespasses to us. He made Him who knew no sin to be sin for us, so that we might become the righteousness of God in Him (2 Corinthians 5:18, 21).

This righteousness of God is far greater than anything you could ever have obtained by good deeds, for no human righteousness equals the righteousness of God!

Often we suffer with a lack of peace because of our self-worth and because our value or significance is threatened. But when you live in the righteousness Jesus has with the Father, you have this assurance deep within your heart that God is with you. You feel no charge against you because the amazing love that Jesus enjoys with the Father provides you with a sense of His value and significance.

Oh what joy to live in this heavenly peace that flows from the righteousness Jesus has with the Father – a righteousness which He now imparts to live in you.

To live in His righteousness on a daily basis you need to have your mind renewed.

You need to learn to think like Jesus, for God has made Jesus your righteousness (1 Corinthians 1:30).

His righteousness is where your heart and mind are one with God and you are conformed to His divine will in purpose, thought, and action (Hebrews 5:13 AMPB).

God gave this righteousness to Abraham simply because he believed.

And He gives it to you when you put your trust in His Son Jesus Christ.

Isn't it wonderful that when you believe in Jesus you are given the righteousness He has with the Father so you can live in His peace – a peace far more wonderful than the human mind can comprehend?

Let's pray: Heavenly Father, You are so wonderful; I love You for giving me the righteousness Jesus has with You in heaven so that I can live in perfect peace.

In Jesus' Name, Amen.

*Fear not, for I am with you; be not dismayed, for I am your God.
I will strengthen you, yes, I will help you, I will uphold you with
My righteous right hand*

Isaiah 41:10

The revelation of the righteousness Jesus has with the Father in
heaven, which He so generously gives and maintains in you, will
drive fear and dismay from your heart.

When Jesus talked about the Life He lives in the righteousness of
God, a Life that knows no sin, He said, 'You shall know the truth
as you will experience this Life for yourself and the truth of this
Life shall make you free from consciousness of sin!' (John 8:32)

Dear child of God, the righteousness Jesus gives enables you to
stand before God with nothing against you, nothing He could
even chide you for (Colossians 1:22).

As the old hymn so beautifully says, 'Jesus paid it all, all to Him
I owe, sin had left a crimson stain, He washed me white as snow!'

So you see, you have nothing to fear from a heavenly Father who
loves you so perfectly that He gives you the Life He has given
Jesus at His throne.

This Life in which Jesus lives in the love of the Father is what He
now gives to you to eliminate all dread of what will happen when
you see Him.

You may say, but what do I do when I feel so very earthly, when
I feel that I am but a mere human being?

Do not be afraid, for you have the Lord Jesus at the throne of God
who is upholding you with His own righteousness.

Trust Jesus; He will never fail to lift your heart to enjoy the Life He has with the Father.

Consider the good work He has already begun in you that you now share His heavenly Life. You can trust Him in whatever area you are still falling short of the glory He has with the Father, because He will perfect this in you also (Philippians 1:6, 4:19).

Now set your sights on the return of Jesus, for when you see Him you will be radiant with His glory (Colossians 3:4).

Let's pray: Heavenly Father, I love You; I trust You; I know I have nothing to fear, for You are upholding me with the righteousness Jesus has with You in heaven. Oh my Father, how I long to see You. I worship You!

In Jesus' Name, Amen.

But now the righteousness of God apart from the law is revealed, being witnessed by the law and the prophets

Romans 3:21

The only place you can live free from consciousness of sin is in the righteousness of God. This life in the righteousness of God is what Jesus communicates by His Spirit. Oh, the glory of the Life He lives in the righteousness of God!

The law and the prophets spoke of this righteousness; it was their dream, their hope and they longed for it as the dear pants for the water.

The great prophet Daniel lived an exemplary life and it was said of him that people couldn't find anything to criticize! He was faithful and honest and made no mistakes. However, this greatly beloved man was not without the same struggles that any man faces as He yearned for this righteousness and cried out, 'O Lord, You are righteous; but as for us, we are always shamefaced with sin, just as You see us now' (Daniel 9:7). Oh how Daniel pleaded with God for mercy, acknowledging that all had failed to keep His laws. As it is written, 'There is none righteous, no, not one' (Romans 3:10).

The Jews, who tried so hard to get right with God by keeping His laws, never succeeded. Why not? They did not understand that Jesus had to die in order to make them right with God. They were trying to make themselves right by keeping the Jewish laws and customs, but that is not God's way of salvation! They did not understand that Jesus, who lives in perfect righteousness with God, gives to those who trust in Him the Life they are trying to get by keeping His laws (Romans 9:31, 10:3-4 LB).

If you could have lived a life free from sin by the law, then God would not have had to give you a different way to get out of the grip of sin. No, the Scriptures insist you are sin's prisoner. The only way out of the grip of sin is through faith in Jesus!

Jesus is the Way of escape for all who believe in Him (Galatians 3:22 LB).

The Life He faithfully gives knows no sin or separation from the love of the Father.

Dear child of God, trust in Jesus and let your heart find rest in the wonderful Life He gives.

Let's pray: Heavenly Father, my heart is overwhelmed that You have given me Your own righteousness in Christ so that I can live in the perfect oneness Jesus has with You in heaven.

In Jesus' Name, Amen.

But now the righteousness of God apart from the law is revealed, being witnessed by the law and the prophets

Romans 3:21

Now you know you are living in the righteousness of God through the Life of Jesus in you. What purpose then does the law serve? The Bible teaches us that it was added in order to make us aware of our transgressions (Galatians 3:19).

The truth is that I would not have known sin except through the law. I would not have known that I was guilty of covetousness unless the law had said, 'You shall not covet' (Romans 7:7).

The law is therefore not made for a righteous person but for the lawless and insubordinate, for the ungodly and for sinners, for the unholy and profane, for murderers, for manslayers, for fornicators, for sodomites, for kidnappers, for liars, for perjurers (1 Timothy 1:8-10).

The Apostle Paul, who was formerly a teacher of the law, said, 'By the law's standard of righteousness I was proven to be blameless and no fault was found in me. But what things were gain to me, these I have counted loss for Christ. Yet indeed I also count all things loss for the excellence of the knowledge of Christ Jesus my Lord, for whom I have suffered the loss of all things, and count them rubbish, that I may gain Christ and be found in Him, not having my own righteousness, which is from the law, but that which is through faith in Christ, the righteousness which is from God by faith (Philippians 3:6-9).

Paul said, 'It was through reading the Scripture that I came to realise that I could never find God's favour by trying and failing to obey His laws. I came to realise that acceptance with God comes by believing in Jesus' (Galatians 2:19 LB).

Let Jesus liberate your heart from the pain of failure! For through the Life He has with the Father, Jesus has the power to free you from sin and give rest to your soul.

Be encouraged, for as the sun shines forth its light and warmth, so Jesus will empower, uphold and enable you, without ceasing, to live the Life He lives in perfect righteousness, peace and joy.

Let's pray: Heavenly Father, thank You for giving me in Jesus everything Your law demands. Your perfect righteousness, peace and joy are wonderful!

In Jesus' Name, Amen.

Do we then make void the law through faith? Certainly not! On the contrary, we establish the law

Romans 3:31

It is sin that causes us to ask the question whether we need to obey the law or not. For the sin nature cannot, nor will ever, obey the law. The law is spiritual, but sin is carnal and demonic. Those who do not have the Life of Jesus in them will always feel condemned by the law because it exposes the sin nature in them. But you have received the Life that Jesus enjoys with the Father. Therefore you have His righteousness to guard your heart and mind. Sin no longer is your master for you are no longer under the law where sin enslaved you, making you feel ashamed, afraid and condemned. The power of sin was broken over you when the Life of Jesus came into your heart.

When you were baptised you became a part of Jesus Christ. Through His death the power of your sinful nature was shattered and your old sin-loving nature was buried with Him. Through His resurrection, you were given His wonderful, sinless Life to live as you rose from the waters of baptism. So now you don't have to be afraid of your old master sin ever again because you are free! For whom the Son sets free is free indeed (John 8:36)!

Your evil desires were nailed to the cross with Jesus. That part of you that loves to sin was crushed and fatally wounded, so that your sin-loving body is no longer under its control. You are no longer a slave of sin, for Christ Jesus, who became sin for you, took all your sins in His own body on the tree. Having died to sin once and for all, He now lives by the power of God to reveal His Life in you.

So say it out loud, 'Thank You Jesus! Sin is no longer my master. Your righteousness is my master and I see the fruit of Your Life in me!' (Romans 6:18).

This is why you are no longer under the law; the righteous requirement of the law is fulfilled in you who live by the power of the Life Jesus has with the Father (Romans 8:4).

Let's pray: Heavenly Father, Your ever-living Word, Jesus Christ, lives in my heart and mind giving me the willingness and ability to please You. I delight myself in Your Word and live in order to be well pleasing to You.

In Jesus' Name, Amen.

Do we then make void the law through faith? Certainly not! On the contrary, we establish the law

Romans 3:31

The Life Jesus lives in the righteousness of God now lives in you, bearing fruit against which there is no law (Galatians 5:22-23).

You are now free. You don't have to be afraid that you are failing God anymore, for it is no longer you who live, but Jesus lives in you and He can never fail. Your ability to please God is Christ in you. Christ in you has made you well pleasing to God. You now live through faith in Him who loves you and gave Himself for you. Jesus completely fulfilled the law and His Spirit in you is your freedom from the law.

So what does this freedom look like? Now that the Life Jesus has with the Father is in you, when you read the law your spirit rejoices because you feel one with God, for when you read the law it bears witness of His Life in you and gives you understanding of the will of God.

For example, when I once read, 'He who stops his ears from hearing of bloodshed, and shuts his eyes from seeing evil: he will dwell on high' (Isaiah 33:15), the Spirit of Christ leapt up in me and gave me understanding, willingness and His ability not to give myself to entertainment in which bloodshed and evil are paraded.

Now my heart and mind withdraw from this kind of entertainment not because I am trying to obey a law, but because the love of Jesus within me compels me.

This is therefore your freedom from the law – Christ's ability to please God.

Jesus Christ is God's ever-living Word in your heart, enabling you to always want what He wants.

His Spirit fills your mind with His thoughts so that you will always know what He wants.

So you see you are no longer under the law but under grace, because you are now dead to sin through the Life of Jesus within.

There is nothing more wonderful than to live the Life Jesus has with the Father and be well pleasing to Him!

Let's pray: Heavenly Father, Your ever-living Word, Jesus Christ lives in my heart and mind and gives me understanding and the willingness and His ability to please You. I delight myself in Your Word and love to be well pleasing to You.

In Jesus' Name, Amen.

What then shall we sin because we are not under law but under grace? Certainly not!

Romans 6:15

Jesus desires what is written in the law to live in your heart and mind by His Spirit.

What did Jesus mean when He said, 'Depart from me, you who practice lawlessness' (Matthew 7:23), and, 'Whoever therefore breaks one of the least of these commandments, and teaches men so, shall be called least in the kingdom of heaven, but whoever does them and teaches them, shall be called great in the kingdom of heaven. For I say to you, that unless your righteousness exceeds the righteousness of the scribes and Pharisees, you will by no means enter the kingdom of heaven?'

Jesus goes on to say that the law says you shall not murder and whoever murders will be in danger of the judgment. 'But I say that if you harbour anger in your heart against your brother without cause you are in danger of judgment.'

He also said, 'You have heard that it was said to those of old, you shall not commit adultery. But I say to you that whoever looks at a woman to lust for her has already committed adultery with her in his heart' (Matthew 5:19-22, 27-28).

Jesus makes it clear that He is looking for more than the righteousness of the Pharisees, who boasted in keeping the Law. Jesus shows that men's best efforts cannot measure up to the glorious Life of living in the righteousness He gives, through which the things that were carved on tablets of stone are now written on your heart and mind by His Spirit.

You can clearly see this in the Apostle Paul's life, who according to the law was a Pharisee, and concerning the righteousness of the law was blameless, yet he counted it but loss and mere rubbish compared to the priceless privilege of knowing Jesus (Philippians 3:5-8).

I pray your heart finds rest in Jesus today as you begin to live in the righteousness He has with the Father and enjoy the power of His Life-giving Word living in your heart and mind to keep you free from sin (2 Peter 1:4).

You will never need to feel the awful pain of failure again, nor suffer the scrutiny of the law, because the Life Jesus gives knows no sin or failure. Through His Life in you, you will delight yourself in the law because it bears witness of His Life in you and makes you feel that you are well pleasing to God.

Let's pray: Heavenly Father, I worship You for Your indescribable gift of grace through the Life of Jesus in me. I thank You that whenever I read the law or the prophets they bear witness to Your wonderful heavenly, holy and sinless Life in me.

In Jesus' Name, Amen.

What then shall we sin because we are not under law but under grace? Certainly not!

Romans 6:15

The righteousness of those who live under the law is compared by the Prophet Isaiah to filthy rags (Isaiah 64:6). The filthy rags referred to here are the clothes on a leper whose flesh has putrefied. While his clothing may seem clean on the outside, they are unclean on the inside because of the corruption of the flesh.

Some people don't realise that God cares about the thoughts of their hearts; while they may come across outwardly as good to others, God looks at their inner life because He cares about what comes from the heart.

When there are evil, angry, lustful thoughts in your heart the law cannot take those away; only Jesus can do that! He broke the power of the sin nature in His death to free you forever from its awful grip, and He rose from the grave to give you forever His Life that reigns over sin and death. Now that is what is meant by living under grace instead of under law! Grace is the Life of Jesus in you empowering you to live victorious over sin.

The Life you now live is nothing but grace upon grace because it is not your own, it is a gift of God; it is the Life of Jesus who loves you and gave Himself for you. How unsearchable are the riches of the glory of His grace, that Jesus gives you His Life to live! This is why you grow in grace as you know Jesus more, and why you will never need to feel barren or unfruitful in your relationship with Him. For by His Spirit in you, you will bear the fruit of His heavenly, holy sinless Life. You will bear the fruit of His love, joy, peace, longsuffering, kindness, goodness, faithfulness, gentleness, self-control, yes every blessing He has with the Father.

When the graces of the Life of Jesus emanate from you, you will discover there is no law against you (Galatians 5:22-23)! In fact, quite the opposite - you will delight yourself in the law day and night as it bears witness to His Life in you.

Remember when Jesus was on the Mount of Transfiguration and Moses, representing the law, and Elijah, representing the prophets, appeared to Him? They both bore witness to Jesus. Then when God appeared, He said, 'This is my beloved Son, in whom I am well pleased. Hear Him!' (Matthew 17:5). So you see, Moses and the prophets are on your side as the Father bears witness to the Life of His Son in you.

Let's pray: Heavenly Father, I worship You for the indescribable gift of Your grace. I thank You that whenever I read the law or prophets they bear witness to the Life Jesus has with You in me.
In Jesus' Name, Amen.

For the law was given through Moses, but grace and truth came through Jesus Christ

John 1:17

The Lord God, who made heaven and earth, remembered His promise to His friend Abraham and came at the set time to visit the children of Israel through Moses in the land of Egypt. The small group of seventy people who had arrived there four hundred years before, had multiplied to some two million, and while they were sorely afflicted as slaves they had adopted strange idols and ungodly ways. When God made Himself known to them, He raised His hand in an oath, saying, 'I am the Lord Your God, each of you throw away the abominations which are before your eyes, and do not defile yourself with the idols of Egypt.' But they rebelled and would not obey.

Then God, wanting to pour out His fury, acted for His name's sake, lest His name would be profaned before the Gentiles. He made His people go out into the wilderness and gave them His laws. If a man obeyed these laws, he would live by them. He also gave them His Sabbath, because He longed for their affection so that they might know, 'I am the Lord who sanctifies you.' But the people of God did not put away their idols from before their eyes and greatly defiled the Sabbath (Ezekiel 20).

Can you see that God gave His laws to turn peoples' hearts from evil and He gave the Sabbath to sanctify their affections? Knowing this it helps you understand, now that the Life of Jesus is in you, why you are under grace and not the law (Romans 6:15; Galatians 3:24). For the law never had the power to liberate anyone from the grip of sin, nor did it have the power to perfect people's affections for God. It only pointed to our need for redemption as it exposed the nature of sin. This is why there were continual burnt offerings and sacrifices for sins which were offered according to the law. But God had no pleasure in these because they were a reminder of sin.

This is why God counts very dear the cross of Jesus, because it is a continual reminder that the price for sin has been paid in full.

You see Jesus, in perfect affection for the Father, gave Himself to take away all our sins. As it is written, we have been sanctified through the offering of the body of Jesus Christ once and for all (Hebrews 10:8-10). Jesus has become your righteousness, sanctification and redemption (1 Corinthians 1:30).

So you have nothing to fear from the law because the grace and truth of the Life of Jesus Christ in you knows no sin or separation from the Father's great love.

Let's pray: Heavenly Father, the more You open my eyes to the grace and truth I have in sharing the Life and blessings Jesus has with You in heaven, the more my heart shouts Your praise.

In Jesus' Name, Amen.

For the law was given through Moses, but grace and truth came through Jesus Christ

John 1:17

It is good and right to take a day of rest and to separate oneself from the business of life in order to enjoy God, family and friends. However the Sabbath, while it honoured God who created all things, also foreshadowed things that were to come in Jesus (Colossians 2:16-17).

Jesus' affection was to do the will of the Father and in doing His will He gave Himself in perfect love as a well-pleasing sacrifice (Hebrews 10:5-10).

In total surrender and love for God, Jesus died as the Passover Lamb during the afternoon of the first Good Friday when He cried, 'It is finished,' and, 'into Your hands I commit My spirit.'

As a man, Jesus rested so to speak on the Sabbath when He died. Then on Sunday morning, He rose triumphantly over sin and death to usher in the new creation in perfect oneness with the Father. For that reason the early church gathered on a Sunday morning – as we do today – to worship God in the Spirit and rejoice in Christ Jesus.

Dearly beloved, can't you see that the law made nothing perfect? While the law was given through Moses, he had to put a veil over his face because the people could not bear to see the glory of God while sin was exposed by the law in their hearts.

However, when you turn to Jesus the veil is taken away because His Spirit in you bears witness to God's grace and truth that there is no law against you. Jesus has set you free from sin and has filled your heart with His love for the Father.

Perhaps you have struggled entering the rest of God because you have sought to love Him in your own strength. Let Jesus draw you up into the Life He lives in the love of the Father and you will never struggle again. This is that perfect rest that the Father longs for you to live in, where it is no longer you who lives but Christ in you.

Simply believe in Jesus. He is able and faithful to keep filling you with His perfect love for the Father and set your heart firmly into the rest He has with the Father.

What grace and truth you are given in the Life Jesus has with the Father! Can there be any other rest prepared for your soul, but to bless the Lord and all that is within you and praise His Holy Name?

Bless the Lord, for nothing will be able to disturb you now Jesus lives in you!

Let's pray: Heavenly Father, You have opened my eyes to the grace and truth of the Life and blessings Jesus has with You in heaven. I will bless the Lord, O my soul; and all that is within me, bless His Holy Name!

In Jesus' Name, Amen.

But we all, with unveiled face, beholding as in a mirror the glory of the Lord, are being transformed into the same image from glory to glory, just as by the Spirit of the Lord

2 Corinthians 3:18

Do we now lay aside the Word of God because we are under grace and not the law? No, on the contrary, we bear witness to the Word of God which was written on tablets of stone but now is written by the Spirit of God on our hearts and minds.

The Word living in the heart and mind of man is perfectly revealed in Jesus, for you can clearly see in Him that the grace and truth of the Life He lived came from the Father.

Now you, who have been born again through the Word of God living in your heart and mind, behold as in a mirror the Life of Christ in you when you read His Word. You see, God's Word perfectly mirrors the Life of Jesus in you and transforms you into His likeness.

Before you knew the Life of Jesus in you, when you read or heard the Word of God you often felt you were falling short of His glory because you were self-conscious instead of Christ-conscious. But now that you have His Life in you (which is the same Spirit of Life who inspired the prophets and apostles to write the Scriptures in the first place) you rejoice in His Word because it bears witness to His Life in you.

It is through the Life of Jesus in you that the Scriptures help you to know, perceive and recognise the only true living God as your Father and you as His child.

Only now that the Life Jesus has with the Father is in you can you truly delight yourself day and night in His Holy, ever-living Word, for it bears witness to His Life in you.

Come dear child of God, and take a good look into the mirror of God's Word and you will see the real you.

You are truly a child of God!

Let's pray: Heavenly Father, I believe in the glory of the Life Jesus has with You. I believe this Life is in me. I believe Your Word mirrors Your Life in me and I believe I am being transformed into Your likeness.

In Jesus' Name, Amen.

But we all, with unveiled face, beholding as in a mirror the glory of the Lord, are being transformed into the same image from glory to glory, just as by the Spirit of the Lord

2 Corinthians 3:18

Now you know, because the Life Jesus has with the Father is in you, that the Word of God perfectly mirrors who you are. But even as the Word mirrors who you are through His Life in you, you have become a mirror of His Life in others.

The more you grow to know the Life of Jesus in you, the more radiant you become as a mirror to reflect His Life in others. This means that while you are with them, they are no longer self-conscious but become conscious of the Life of Jesus in them. They feel completely accepted and loved by Him; they feel no charge or condemnation from Him; they realise that they are holy and well pleasing in His sight, because you mirror their new nature.

Oh dear child of God, can't you see the riches of the glory of His grace? Does not this truth liberate you to live in unbroken fellowship with the Father and the Son so that in nothing you will fall short of His glory, but that in all you are, say and do the Life Jesus has with the Father is revealed in you?

Jesus prayed, 'Father the same glory You gave Me, the glory of being one with You, I have given them so that the world may know You sent Me and have loved them as much as You have loved Me. Father the world does not know You but I know You and these whom You have given Me out of the world they know You sent Me because I have revealed You to them and will keep on revealing You to them so that the same love with which You loved Me may be in them and I in them' (John 17:22-26).

Can you see how richly blessed you are because the Life Jesus has with the Father is in you?

The whole Word of God, from Genesis to Revelation, mirrors His Life in you.

Through His Life and love in you, you have become a mirror for others to see His Life in them.

This is Jesus!

This is Christianity! This is you!

Let's pray: Heavenly Father, thank You for loving me as You love Jesus. I love Your Word because it helps me to see Your Life in me. I long for Your Life in me to help others know how much You love them.

In Jesus' Name, Amen.

Therefore, from now on, we regard no one according to the flesh. Even though we have known Christ according to the flesh, yet now we know Him thus no longer

2 Corinthians 5:16

Jesus said, 'That which is born of the flesh is flesh, and that which is born of the Spirit is spirit' (John 3:6). This shows that even though you are human and earthly, God in His great love has given you the privilege of sharing in the Life of Jesus. This is why the Scripture says anyone who is in Christ is a new creation (2 Corinthians 5:17).

Now that you know the Life of Jesus in you, learn to recognise Him in others! To recognise what people are like after the flesh is earthly, but to know others as they are known by God is heavenly. When Jesus asked His disciples who they thought He was, Peter replied, 'You are the Christ, the Son of the living God.' Jesus said, 'Blessed are you, for no one has revealed this to you, but My Father in heaven' (Matthew 16).

Jesus said, 'It is written in the prophets, 'they shall all be taught by God.' Therefore everyone who has heard and learned from the Father comes to me' (John 6:45).

Now that you have the Life Jesus has with the Father, the Holy Spirit yearns in you with jealousy that you may be fully clothed with His heavenly Life, so that your earthly nature may be completely hidden in Him (Colossians 3:3-4).

Be greatly encouraged, dear child of God, for this is the wonderful plan and purpose of the Father for you. He longs for you to know - through personal experience - the love Jesus lives in at His throne, which far surpasses mere knowledge without experience, so that you may be filled throughout your whole being with all the fullness He has with the Father, and that you may have the richest measure of His divine Presence, becoming in spirit, soul and body wholly filled and flooded with God Himself!

You may say, 'How is this possible, for I am so human and so earthly?' Believe in Jesus, for the Life He has with the Father is powerfully working in you, by which He is able to carry out His purpose and do superabundantly far over and above all that you dare ask or think, infinitely beyond your highest prayers, desires, thoughts, hopes, or dreams.

Now to God be the glory through Jesus Christ in you forever and ever, Amen!

Let's pray: Heavenly Father, I long to be fully clothed with Your heavenly nature so all may see Your Life in me. Help me look at others the way You do and to love them with Your love.

In Jesus' Name, Amen.

And all who sat in the council, looking steadfastly at him, saw his face as the face of an angel

Acts 6:15

The glory of the heavenly Life of Jesus is for you as surely as Jesus' death is for you.

You may say, 'Yes, I believe Jesus died for me, but I don't see His Life in me; all I see is myself and my weaknesses. I feel so human and far away from His heavenly Life.' This, dear child of God, is the most common temptation we all experience. Think about Jesus; even while being led by the Holy Spirit, Satan tempted Him to disbelieve that He was the Son of God. Jesus had to resist him by saying, 'It is written, man shall not live by bread alone, but by every word of God' (Luke 3:21-22, 4:4).

You see you will grow strong in the Life Jesus has with the Father by feeding on His Word. Jesus said, 'I am the bread of Life, he who comes to Me shall never hunger, and he who believes in Me shall never thirst.' 'As the living Father sent Me and I live because of the Father, so he who feeds on Me will live because of Me' (John. 6:35, 57).

The reason you are self-conscious instead of Christ-conscious is because you are hungry; you need to be fed with the Life Jesus has with the Father!

Be greatly encouraged, for God who is faithful will Himself feed you with the Life of His Son so that you will be utterly satisfied.

The reason Stephen's face shone like that of an angel was because he was filled with the Life of Jesus. The darker it became, the more he shone with heaven's glory, until he saw Jesus standing at the right hand of God. Oh, how Jesus longs for you to be fully satisfied with His heavenly Life and shine forth with His glory.

Don't be weary with yourself when you feel weak or powerless; begin to encourage yourself in Jesus, trust in Him, delight yourself in Him and meditate on this, that it is the work of His grace to draw you up into the Life He has with the Father.

This Life with the Father is your daily food and drink.

Jesus said, 'If anyone thirsts, let him come to Me and drink. He who believes in Me, as the Scripture has said, out of his heart will flow rivers of living water' (John 7:37-38).

Let's pray: Heavenly Father, I thank You for giving me this day my daily bread and satisfying me with the Life Jesus has with You in heaven so that I may be radiant with Your glory.

In Jesus' Name, Amen.

Being justified freely by His grace through the redemption that is in Christ Jesus

Romans 3:24

God has more in mind for you than to save you from sin; He longs to bring you into the Life and blessings Jesus has in heaven.

You may say, 'Sure, I believe I will go to heaven.' But do you believe that the Father longs to reveal the Life of His Son in you here on earth, so that everyone who meets you believes He sent Jesus and loves you as much as He loves Him?

'But where do I begin?' your hungry soul may cry. You begin at the cross where Jesus died for you. He bore the awful punishment of God's wrath against all your sins and paid for you the full ransom in His precious blood.

Now, because of what Jesus has done by dying for you, God is pleased to declare you not guilty of offending Him and justifies you freely by His grace.

So believe the truth and forever live free to enjoy the love of the Father. For who shall lay a charge against you when God Himself has justified you? Who can condemn you when Jesus died for you and is raised from the dead, ever-living to impart His heavenly Life?

There is nothing that can separate you from God's love, for the Life of Jesus now lives in you. Come, dear child of God, and draw near to the Father, for you will find His mercy to help you receive all the grace you need for living a truly godly life.

Now these are the riches of the glory of His grace, not only to justify you freely by His grace, but to give you His Life to enjoy.

What glory to stand in this place of His amazing grace and see Him work His Life in you with all the rich blessings of heaven!

Let's pray: Heavenly Father, here I stand in Your presence, lifting holy hands to You. I am singing Your praise for You have justified me freely by Your grace so I may enjoy Your Love forever and ever.

In Jesus' Name, Amen.

To the praise of the glory of His grace, by which He made us accepted in the Beloved

Ephesians 1:6

Now lift your hands in praise. Give thanks for the glory of God's grace that you can now stand before His face without shame or blame, holy, acceptable and well-pleasing in His sight.

I pray this revelation of the glory of His grace fills you - spirit, soul and body - so you will never look down on yourself again but will always give thanks for His amazing grace, for this is the will of God in Christ Jesus for you (1 Thessalonians 5:18).

Think about this: you have been made accepted in the Beloved!

Jesus has made you well-pleasing to God; He has removed every charge against you; He has fully cleared your record and because of His Life in you, you are no longer under condemnation.

Through the Life of Jesus the Beloved, you have been given the richest measure of God's grace so you may obtain the highest amount of present happiness and the fullest reward in glory.

Oh, how it pleases the Father to see His grace multiply in you so you will never feel barren or unfruitful in your union with Jesus but will always see His Life in you.

Make this confession and say, 'The Life I now live is the Life Jesus has with the Father; the fruit I now bear comes from His Life at the throne of God; I am blessed, I am heavenly blessed!'

You see, this is the faith of the Son of God taking root in your heart. You are learning to think like Him, believe like Him and live like Him.

For even as Jesus the Beloved lives at the throne, so you have been brought into the very presence of God through His Life in you and you are now standing before Him with nothing against you.

You are loved with the same love the Father loves Jesus.

Let's pray: Heavenly Father, You are worthy, You are worthy oh Lord, to receive glory, honour and power forever and ever.

In Jesus' Name, Amen.

In Him we have redemption through His blood, the forgiveness of sins, according to the riches of His grace

Ephesians 1:7

When you think of the riches of His grace you need to realise the worth of those riches because you have not been redeemed with such corruptible things as silver or gold but with the precious blood of Jesus.

When Adam and Eve suffered the pain of separation from God it was because sin made them self-conscious as the glory of His Life faded away. So for Adam and his wife, the Lord God made tunics of skin, and clothed them (Genesis 3:21).

You see, God clothed their nakedness - their 'self-consciousness' - with the skin of an animal whose blood was shed to cover them. This is what became known as 'to make atonement', which means 'to cover, pacify or appease.' King David, who knew what this meant from personal experience, said, 'Blessed is he whose transgression is forgiven, whose sin is covered' (Psalm 32:1).

While these sacrifices were but a shadow of the good things to come, God gave them for those who sought His forgiveness and did not punish them as they deserved, for He was looking forward to the time when Jesus would come to take away all sins for all time.

So while you are thinking about the riches of His grace, look to Jesus who gave up His glory as God and became the Son of Man, our Saviour, the Lamb of God who takes away the sin of the world (John 1:29).

When Jesus gave Himself to God for our sins as one sacrifice for all time, His love for us was like sweet perfume to the Father.

By that one offering of Himself He forever made perfect in the sight of God all those whom He makes holy through His Life in them.

You see, through the shedding of His innocent blood Jesus became the mercy seat of God.

This is why Jesus has the right to forgive you, justify you freely, give you the Holy Spirit who proceeds from the Father - washing you with His blood so that you are continually renewed and regenerated by His Life in you - and enable you to stay in fellowship with the Father, free from sin, until He returns.

Is there greater treasure than this?

Let's pray: Heavenly Father, I lift my hands and give You praise for the riches of the glory of Your grace.

In Jesus' Name, Amen.

But by the grace of God I am what I am, and His grace toward me was not in vain; but I laboured more abundantly than they all, yet not I, but the grace of God which was with me
1 Corinthians 15:10

Now you have begun to discover the riches of the glory of His grace. I say 'begun' because with every new discovery you realise there is so much more to see of the Life Jesus has with the Father revealed in you.

When the great prophet Isaiah was caught up in the Spirit and saw the glory Jesus has with the Father he said, 'Lord, who has believed our report? And to whom has the arm of the Lord been revealed?' (John 12:38). In other words, Isaiah said, 'Lord, even if I give them Your miracles as proof, who will believe me when I tell them of this heavenly Life?'

John the Baptist said, 'He has come from heaven, He tells what He has seen and heard, but how few believe what He tells them!' (John 3:31-32 LB).

John, the beloved Apostle, said about Jesus, 'The Life was manifested, and we have seen, and bear witness, and declare to you that eternal Life which was with the Father and was manifested to us' (1 John 1:2).

You see this is the work of His grace, that the Life Jesus has with the Father is revealed in you.

When the Apostle Paul says, 'I am what I am by the grace of God,' what he is saying is, 'Despite the fact that I am human, the Life I now live is the Life of Jesus the Son of God in me.'

Then he adds, 'I did not receive this grace in vain, this Life is not just for me but, just like Jesus - who went about doing good sharing His life - so I am a witness of His Life.'

Can you see how rich God has made you in Jesus, that He even shares His own heavenly Life with you and has made you a partaker of His Divine Nature, of His own character, goodness and glory?

The more you begin to share His Life with others the more you will realise how rich you are, until His grace becomes a powerful river of His Life and love flowing through you.

Let's pray: Heavenly Father, You have made me in Jesus what I am by Your grace. I thank You that I may bear witness of Your Life and love.

In Jesus' Name, Amen.

But by the grace of God I am what I am, and His grace toward me was not in vain; but I laboured more abundantly than they all, yet not I, but the grace of God which was with me

1 Corinthians 15:10

There is a story of a man who travelled on an old steam ship from England to America. He had just enough money for a ticket, so he survived in the cold outside, eating cheese and crackers as he looked through the window seeing others enjoying the journey. When New York came into view, he was asked, 'Why are you not inside enjoying all the good things?' He said, 'I am not a stowaway; I have a ticket. Here it is.' As he looked at it, he saw to his amazement that the ticket entitled him to every benefit on board the ship.

Jesus is the only ticket to heaven, but do you realise that He entitles you to every blessing!

How we praise God, the Father of our Lord Jesus Christ, who has blessed us with every blessing in heaven because we belong to Jesus Christ. You have everything when you have Christ, and you are filled with God through your union with Him (Colossians 2:10 LB).

When Jesus looked at His Church, as we read in Revelation 3:14-20, He expressed great concern that they were neither cold nor hot but lukewarm. Because they had so much of the passing things of earth they thought they had no need for the heavenly blessings. So Jesus said, 'Return to Me to have your eyes opened to all that is yours in Me, so that you may be clothed with My divine nature and rediscover My heavenly Life in you as the true treasure worth living for.'

Now consider the grace you have received in Jesus and He will anoint your eyes to see, clothe you with His majesty, and fill you with His wonderful heavenly Life.

Begin to sing, 'Turn your eyes upon Jesus, look full in His wonderful face, and the things of earth will grow strangely dim, in the light of His glory and grace.'

Let's pray: Heavenly Father, Your Word says, 'They looked to Him and were radiant, and their faces were not ashamed' (Psalm 34:5). Father, I lift my eyes to You and worship You for Your goodness and grace.

In Jesus' Name, Amen.

But by the grace of God I am what I am, and His grace toward me was not in vain; but I laboured more abundantly than they all, yet not I, but the grace of God which was with me
1 Corinthians 15:10

The truth that it is not our ability but God's grace can be clearly seen in the calling of God's humble servant Moses.

Moses argued that he was not able to speak, but God said, 'Who has made man's mouth? Now therefore, go, and I will be with your mouth and teach you what you shall say' (Exodus 4:10,12).

After this we see that it was God's anointing that enabled Moses to speak His words. That is why whatever Moses said happened! The people said to Moses, 'You go near and hear all that the Lord our God may say, and tell us and we will hear and do it.' (Exodus 5:27) It so pleased God that they were willing to listen to the one through whom He spoke that He promised to bless them if they did what He said. Oh, how God longs for you to hear His word and do what He says so that you may be blessed and become a source of His blessings (Hebrews 4:7).

We see this grace in Jesus who spoke the Word of God. Every word He spoke came from heaven and was filled with Life and love. Jesus said, 'The words I speak to you I do not speak on My own authority; but the Father who dwells in Me does the works' (John 14:10).

Jesus lived so deeply in the grace of God that His whole being knew no separation, no sin. He said, 'He who speaks from himself seeks his own glory; but he who seeks the glory of the One who sent Him is true, and no unrighteousness is in Him' (John 7:18).

Jesus also said, 'I and my Father are one' (John 10:30).

God would have you live in such oneness with Him through the Life of Jesus in you that you learn to think, believe, speak and act like Him.

The Apostle Paul said, 'I would never dare think anything comes from myself, my ability is from God' (2 Corinthians.3:5) – or in other words, 'Not I, but the grace of God that is with me!'

Now dear child of God, let your joy be full and say, 'Not I, but the grace of God!'

Let's pray: Heavenly Father, not I, but Your grace is sufficient that in nothing I will fall short of Your glory but in all I am, say and do, You will be glorified.

In Jesus' Name, Amen.

You have become estranged from Christ, you who attempt to be justified by law; you have fallen from grace

Galatians 5:4

Is it possible, when you have lived the Life Jesus has with the Father and tasted the heavenly blessings, that you would seek your life in anything but Jesus? Remember what He did for you when you heard the good news about how to be saved; how when you put your trust in Jesus He marked you as belonging to Him by giving you the Holy Spirit. Remember how His heavenly Life helped you find and know the only true living God as your Father. Remember how happy you were to sing His praise when He forgave your sins and filled you with His great love.

So how is it possible that you would rather seek to live by the law than by God's amazing grace through faith in Jesus Christ?

Don't you know that those who lived under the law could never secure the assurance Jesus gives? Why? Because no matter how hard they tried to obey God's commands, they failed because of their weak human nature. But you have not so learned Christ. He never fails! He is your unshakable foundation for eternal life for He can never die. He is your freedom from sin for He cannot sin. No matter how much you may groan at times with the pains of your human nature, even if you feel completely dead and powerless to save yourself, you know the Life you now live you live by faith in the Son of God who loves you and gave Himself for you.

Be encouraged, dear child of God, for the Holy Spirit's presence within you has given you a share in the Life Jesus has with the Father. The fact that His life is producing fruit in your life shows you are now free from sin. So trust Jesus, for He is able to keep you from falling and present you faultless in the presence of His glory.

You may say, 'But what do I do when I feel all is lost and gone; when I have made too many mistakes?' Humble yourself under the mighty hand of God and you will find renewed grace. Learn to cast all your care upon Jesus for He cares for you!

You may say, 'But what do I do about these things that are still not right in my life?' Trust Jesus who has started a good work in you to perfect you.

You may say, 'Yes, but I have tried that before and I only endure for a little and then stumble again.' What you need is to let your roots of faith grow deeper and deeper in His love for you, so that you may daily draw your strength from your union with Him and know that, no matter what, Jesus never fails; He will never leave you; He is upholding you with His own righteousness.

Let's pray: Heavenly Father, I humble my heart before You, I know You love me. I know You are with me. I know I can trust You.

In Jesus' Name, Amen.

And He said to me, 'My grace is sufficient for you, for My strength is made perfect in weakness.' Therefore most gladly I will rather boast in my infirmities, that the power of Christ may rest upon me

2 Corinthians 12:9

Now that you know you are what you are by the grace of God, you also know that you have not fallen from grace.

So let your soul arise in the faith of Jesus the Beloved, trust in Him and you will see that the riches of the glory of His grace are more than sufficient, no matter how weak you are.

If you suffer the pains of your weak human nature, begin to rejoice in Jesus who is interceding for you at the throne of God to empower you with His Life.

Again I say, rejoice in Jesus and the power of His Life will be your strength and song in the heat of the battle.

This is all about faith. For even though you are weak and may feel completely powerless, you have faith, and not just any faith. The faith I am talking about is the kind of faith that Jesus Christ our God and Saviour gives. When you first heard the good news of Jesus and God's Word entered your heart, the faith of Jesus the Son of God was created in you.

So when Jesus says, 'My grace is sufficient for you', He is saying, 'All that is mine here in heaven is yours! Even as I have overcome and do the will of my Father, so will you!'

This is one of the most wonderful revelations your tender heart can conceive - that all His mighty resources as both Lord and Christ are now yours. Therefore you need never be afraid of being weak; no, rather rejoice in your weakness for when you are weak, because of His sufficient grace, the power of His Life will manifest in you, so that you may know 'it is no longer I who live, but Christ lives in me' (Galatians 2:20).

Now let the weak say 'I am strong!' (Joel 3:10). 'I can do all things through Christ who strengthens me' (Philippians 4:13).

As the faith of Jesus grows in you, so your mind will be renewed by the Word of God to think, talk and act like Him.

Let's pray: Heavenly Father, You are my light and my salvation; whom shall I fear? You are the strength of my life. Of whom shall I be afraid?

In Jesus' Name, Amen.

And He said to me, 'My grace is sufficient for you, for My strength is made perfect in weakness'. Therefore most gladly I will rather boast in my infirmities, that the power of Christ may rest upon me

2 Corinthians 12:9

Is it possible that anyone would rather boast in their own strength than that of Christ Jesus our Lord?

Tragically, this is not only possible but common.

Think about the Apostle Peter. He was convinced in himself he would never deny Jesus. Not until he suffered the pain of his own weak human nature did he realise that only by grace was he able to be a witness of Jesus.

Think about Abraham and Sarah, who faced the hopelessness of their bodies being as good as dead as they were very old, but kept believing and therefore were given hope against all hope that what God had spoken He would perform. For Abraham and Sarah this life of faith opened their hearts to a wonderful friendship with God and His all-sufficiency.

Think about the Apostle Paul who said, 'I think you ought to know the hard times we went through. We were really crushed and over- whelmed, and feared we would never live through it. We felt we were doomed to die and saw how powerless we were to help ourselves; but that was good, for then we put everything into the hands of God, who alone could save us, for He can even raise the dead. And He did help us, and saved us from a terrible death; Yes, and we expect Him to do it again and again' (2 Corinthians. 1:8-10 LB).

Renewed strength comes to those who expectantly wait on the Lord. King David said, 'I would have lost heart, unless I had believed that I would see the goodness of the Lord in the land of the living. Wait on the Lord; be of good courage, and He shall strengthen your heart; wait, I say, on the Lord!' (Psalm 27:13-14).

It is only through faith in God's grace that you will see the strength of the Life of Jesus in you.

When you look to Jesus who has given you this faith, you will begin to soar to new heights of the strength and power of His Life with the Father. Never limit God by limiting yourself, for no matter how weak you are God's grace is greater.

Let's pray: Heavenly Father, I believe in the unlimited resources of Your supply. I believe Your grace is sufficient. I believe the power of Jesus Christ is me.

In Jesus' Name, Amen.

And He said to me, 'My grace is sufficient for you, for My strength is made perfect in weakness.' Therefore most gladly I will rather boast in my infirmities, that the power of Christ may rest upon me.

2 Corinthians 12:9

Now that you know the blessings of the Life Jesus has with the Father, you know nothing else can satisfy and make you whole. This is why we would rather boast in our infirmities so that the power of Christ's heavenly Life may rest on us.

When all you knew was your own strength, the satisfaction you found was like grasping for the wind; it never lasted. But the Life Jesus gives is like a fountain that springs up in you with eternal Life; this is true living and total satisfaction.

Katharine Kuhlman, a woman of God, overflowed with His Life and became a blessing to multitudes while she had but a very frail body. She discovered that God was not looking for a special kind of vessel; she said, 'All He desires is a yielded vessel.'

Dear child of God, do not be afraid of being weak; don't look down on yourself; don't compare yourself to another and feel inferior. You know God is your Father; He loves you! Learn to think like Jesus. He lived in harmony with the Father and knew the Life He lived came from Him.

There is a market for every kind of satisfaction in the world. My father once said to me, 'Son, not everything that sparkles is gold; keep your eyes on Jesus!' We should never forget that our lives are worth more than all earthly pleasures, when Jesus shed His own precious blood to purchase us and give us His wonderful heavenly Life to live.

God made everything on earth so beautiful, and it is your relationship with Jesus and His Life in you that makes everything enjoyable.

If life on earth seems empty and useless, come to Jesus and let His power rest on you. Just as the bright morning sun gives light, colour and beauty, so you will see everything come alive and become fun again.

Let's pray: Heavenly Father, You are the reason for living and You give meaning and value to everything. Thank You for filling me with Your Life and love.

In Jesus' Name, Amen.

And of His fullness we have all received, and grace for grace
John 1:16

From the fullness of His Life with the Father, Jesus gives you one blessing after another. This is why the Holy Spirit enables you never to stop thanking God for all the wonderful gifts He gives. Now that you are Christ's, the Father has enriched your whole life!

You see every grace and blessing, every spiritual gift and power for doing His will during this time of waiting for the return of Jesus Christ, are yours in Him.

Meditate on this, that God meets all your needs according to the riches of His glory by Christ Jesus! (Philippians 4:19).

What God has given Jesus at His throne He now gives to you by the Holy Spirit, so that in nothing you will come short of anything you need for living a truly godly life. Jesus said, 'What I do you will do also, because I go to the Father' (John 14:12).

So if you feel you come short in any area, trust Jesus to enable you. There is no good gift He will withhold from you; as it is written, 'The Lord will give grace and glory; no good thing will He withhold from those who walk uprightly' (Psalm 84:11).

So draw near to God in full assurance of faith, like the leper who came to Jesus and said, 'If You are willing, You can make me clean.' Then Jesus, moved with compassion, stretched out His hand and touched him, and said, 'I am willing; be cleansed.' Immediately the leprosy left him! (Mark 1:40-42).

Can you see how willing Jesus is to meet your needs? So begin to bless Jesus with all your soul for all His wonderful gifts, for He is willing and well able to forgive all your sins, heal all your diseases and crown you with the Life He has with the Father.

As you sing His praises you will discover His gifts will keep coming and never stop, for there is no end to the goodness of His great love for you.

Let's pray: Heavenly Father, I love You! You are so good to me! I believe I will never lack for I live in the overflow of Your goodness and grace.

In Jesus' Name, Amen.

I thank my God always concerning you for the grace which was given to you by Christ Jesus, that you were enriched in everything by Him in all utterance and all knowledge

1 Corinthians 1:4-5

I pray your heart is filled with gratitude for the grace that enables you to now live out of the rich treasury of the glory Jesus has with the Father. The resources of the glory of His Life are endless; there is no limitation in His love for you!

Consider how low sin had brought the human heart that man would rather worship the creation than the Creator. Even though they knew God, men and women did not glorify Him as God, nor were they thankful, but became futile in their thoughts and their foolish hearts were darkened. Professing to be wise, they became fools, and changed the glory of the incorruptible God into an image made like corruptible man (Romans 1:21-23).

When all you worship is self and the passing pleasures of this temporal life, it can all be so hopeless and feel so lonely, without God in a very big universe. But oh the riches of the glory of God's grace with which Jesus Christ fills your heart when you begin to realise that He who made the heavens and earth is your Father and that you are enriched with everything by Him.

It is one thing to realise what a horrible deep pit Jesus has saved you from. It is quite another thing to know the blessings of His Life with the Father!

Without Jesus it is impossible to imagine what this Life in fellowship with the Father is like.

Praise Jesus, for the grace and truth of His Life with the Father has come!

No one has seen the Father except Jesus who came forth from the Father to reveal Him (John 1:18).

Jesus shines forth with the Life He has with the Father, for He is the express image of His person, to help you find and know the only true living God (1 John 5:20).

Jesus prayed, 'This is eternal Life that they may know You the only true God, and Jesus Christ whom You have sent' (John 17:3).

I praise You Jesus that Your life is in me.

Let's pray: Heavenly Father, I thank You and praise You for the grace and truth You have given me in Jesus. I am so grateful You have enriched me with Your Life.

In Jesus' Name, Amen.

Who being the brightness of His glory and the express image of His person, and upholding all things by the word of His power, when He had by Himself purged our sins, sat down at the right hand of the Majesty on high

Hebrews 1:3

Remember how Jesus said to His disciples, 'But now I go to Him who sent me. Nevertheless I tell you the truth. It is to your advantage that I go away; for if I do not go away, the Helper will not come to you; but if I depart, I will send Him to you' (John 16:5-7).

How you need to hear this again and again so that your faith in Jesus can become strong and immovable, no matter how human you may feel or what challenges you may face.

After Jesus established the cleansing of your sins, He sat down at the right hand of God to impart the Holy Spirit. So, like the Apostle Paul in Ephesians 3, you may bow your knee before His throne, knowing He will grant you out of the rich treasury of His glory to be strengthened through His Spirit in your innermost being so that you may have the faith to apprehend and enjoy the Life He has with the Father and come to see, together with all other believers, His great love, which is far more wonderful than the human mind can comprehend without the help of the Holy Spirit.

Can you see why Jesus is called Wonderful, Counsellor, Mighty God, Everlasting Father, Prince of Peace (Isaiah 9:6)? He is at the throne of God to communicate the Life He has with the Father. Now through the work of His grace He is drawing you up into the Life He has with the Father so you may experience all its unlimited blessings.

Oh dear child of God, magnify the Lord Jesus with me, and let us exalt His Name together.

Taste and see that He is good.

His blessings overflow in you as you trust in Him!

Let's pray: Heavenly Father, how good You are to me to give me the Life and love Jesus has with You in heaven. Help me through the Holy Spirit to overflow with Your Life and love. I long to see Your name glorified.

In Jesus' Name, Amen.

Blessed be the God and Father of our Lord Jesus Christ, the Father of mercies and God of all comfort

2 Corinthians 1:3

Jesus said, 'When the Comforter comes, whom I shall send to you from the Father, the Spirit of truth who proceeds from the Father, He will testify of Me' (John 15:26).

You see, the Holy Spirit comes forth from the Father's tender heart of mercy. This is why His Spirit comforts and softens your heart.

King David learned through prayer and praise to access God's tender mercies and find comfort so that he too could be tender hearted. He said, 'Though I am surrounded by troubles, You will bring me safely through them' (Psalm 138:7 LB).

Can you see David's tender, trusting heart? This why God said, 'He is a man after my own heart, who will do all my will' (Acts 13:22).

When Israel travelled through the wilderness to the Promised Land, God's Spirit laboured to give them a tender heart of faith. But every time they faced challenges their hearts became hard with discontent, fear and unbelief.

When your heart is hardened your understanding is blinded to the divine flow of God's Spirit. But the moment His Spirit comforts and softens your heart, the river of His Life and blessings begins to flow.

Think about Jesus, who desired to do God's will and gave His Life for us. How He sweat great drops of blood as He wept aloud in prayer to the Father and was comforted by the Holy Spirit (Hebrews 5:7, 9:14). When God saw His tender heart and sweet soul as He pleaded for our forgiveness He was well pleased (Isaiah 53:11).

Now look at the immeasurable blessings without end that flow through Jesus.

With these thoughts begin to sing, 'Great is Your faithfulness, oh God my Father, morning by morning new mercies I see; all I have needed Your hand has provided. Great is Your faithfulness, oh Lord to me!'

Let's pray: Heavenly Father, create in me a tender, trusting heart by the comfort of the Holy Spirit so that Your river of Life and blessings can flow through me.

In Jesus' Name, Amen.

The Lord will perfect that which concerns me; Your mercy, O Lord, endures forever. Do not forsake the work of Your hands
Psalm 138:8

How this Psalm has helped me over the years when it seemed what God intended and planned would never happen and all I could see was my human weaknesses. But now I can see God is faithful, for the good work He has started in us through Jesus He will complete.

Think about Abraham; God said, in Genesis 12:2, 'I will make you.' Then some twenty five years later God said to him in Genesis 17:5, 'I have made you.' By hearing God's Word, Abraham developed a strong friendship with God as He learned to live by faith and give God praise that what He had spoken He was able to perform.

God is able to perform His Word in your life, for you are His workmanship, created in Christ Jesus for good works, which He prepared for you (Ephesians 2:10).

Let the comfort and exhortation of the Scriptures strengthen your faith. Know that God's Word will never return void but will accomplish that for which it was sent (Isaiah 55:11). Know that He will not abandon you for you are the work of His hands. 'But now, O Lord, You are our Father; we are the clay, and You our potter and all we are the work of Your hand' (Isaiah 64:8). 'The Lord, He is God; it is He who has made us, and not we ourselves' (Psalm 100:3).

King David said, 'I will praise You, for I am fearfully and wonderfully made. Marvellous are Your works, and that my soul knows very well' (Psalm 139:14).

Consider the life of David; God made him a man after His own heart – a man who would do all His will. God loved David so much He was pleased for His Son to be called 'the Son of David.' David prayed, 'O Lord God, why have You showered Your blessings on such an insignificant person as I am? Oh, Lord God, what can I say? For You know what I am like! You are doing all these things just because You promised to and because You want to! How great You are!' (2 Samuel 7:18-21 LB). 'My success, at which so many stand amazed, is because of You; I will praise and honour You, O God, for all that You have done for me' (Psalm 71:7-8 LB).

Let's never limit the Almighty by limiting ourselves but together with David say, 'Here I am Lord, I delight to do Your will for Your Word is in my heart' (Psalm 40:8).

Let's pray: Heavenly Father, here I am in Your presence, lifting holy hands to You, singing praises for all You have brought me through, for You are my maker and I love You Father.

In Jesus' Name, Amen.

And the Holy Spirit descended in bodily form like a dove upon Him, and a voice came from heaven which said, 'You are My beloved Son; in You I am well pleased'

Luke 3:22

God wants you to know that you are known by Him. For the solid foundation of God stands with this seal engraved on it: 'The Lord knows those who are His' (2 Timothy 2:19).

The Father said, 'You are my Son; today I have begotten You' (Hebrews 5:5). The Father knew Jesus His Son because the Life He lived came forth from the Father. The beloved Apostle John writes, 'The Life was manifested and we have seen, and bear witness, and declare to you that eternal Life which was with the Father and was manifested to us' (1 John 1:2).

This is why Jesus said, 'I have come down from heaven.' (John 6:42) 'I proceeded forth and came from God' (John 8:42). 'I know where I came from and where I am going. I am with the Father. If you had known Me, you would have known My Father also' (John 8:14, 16, 18). 'He who has seen Me has seen the Father. I am in the Father, and the Father is in Me' (John 14:9-10).

Can you see the glory Jesus has with the Father, that even though He is man in flesh and blood He is known by the Father through His life in Him?

It is this Life and love Jesus has with the Father that He now reveals in you, so that you may know you are known of God. This is what Jesus meant when He said, 'You will know I am in the Father and you in Me, and I in you' (John 14:20).

Now this is how you know you are known by God - by the Life of His Son in you!

You have the witness of the Father in you for He has revealed His Son in you.

And this is also how you know you have eternal Life - through the Life of His Son in you (1 John 5:9-12).

Jesus knew who He was because the Life He lived came forth from the Father.

Dear child of God, the Father longs for you to live in the light of His Life, where Jesus is, and know who you are even as you are known by Him (1 Corinthians 13:12).

Let's pray: Heavenly Father, this is the solid foundation upon which I stand; I know You love me because You have given me eternal Life in Jesus. Thank You Father for the Life and love of Your Son in me.

In Jesus' Name, Amen.

Examine yourselves as to whether you are in the faith. Test yourselves. Do you not know yourselves, that Jesus Christ is in you? Unless indeed you are disqualified

2 Corinthians 13:5

When you became a Christian you became a brand new person on the inside. This is what it means to be born again! The Life Jesus has with the Father is born in you! Through His Life in you a transformation takes place as you are transformed into His likeness.

While there is an instant change when the ever-living Word of God enters your heart, you must also understand that this is just the start of a daily walk with Jesus, where you come to know Him in you and you in Him, as you begin to bear the fruits of His Life.

The Holy Spirit helps you in all of this because He bears witness with your spirit that you are a child of God. He helps you to learn to love yourself because through His blessed presence in you, you will feel the Father's great love for you.

God would have you live in such harmony with Him that you learn to think like Him, believe, talk and act like Him, so that you lose the identity of sin which made you feel separated from Him.

God wants you to know He is one with you and loves you as much as He loves Jesus.

Now consider how great a love the Father has bestowed on you that you are called a child of God!

So you see you do know who you really are, because the Life you now live in your body is the Life Jesus has with the Father.

Therefore you are a child of God!

Let's pray: Heavenly Father, thank You for the faith that Jesus is in me and that as Your child I share the Life He has with You.

In Jesus' Name, Amen.

Examine yourself as to whether you are in the faith. Test yourselves. Do you not know yourselves, that Jesus Christ is in you? Unless indeed you are disqualified

2 Corinthians 13:5

One of the repeated concerns of Christ's apostles was that the Church would not depart from the faith - the faith that they have Life in Christ Jesus by God's grace.

At the end of one of the great epistles, the Apostle Paul wrote to the church of Corinth and said, 'I am jealous for you with godly jealousy. For I have betrothed you to one husband, that I may present you as a chaste virgin to Christ. But I fear, lest somehow, as the serpent deceived Eve by his craftiness, so your minds may be corrupted from the simplicity that is in Christ. For if he who comes preaching another Jesus whom we have not preached, or if you receive a different spirit which you have not received, or a different gospel which you have not accepted - you may well put up with it!' (2 Corinthians 11:2-4).

Paul was a man who examined himself and called his congregations to do the same. You may ask, 'What is this self-examination?'

Remember when you heard the Good News of how to be saved and believed in Jesus, how you were marked as belonging to Him by the Holy Spirit. His blessed presence in you is God's guarantee that He will give you all He has promised. The Holy Spirit's seal upon you means that you can know for sure that God has already purchased you and guarantees to bring you to Himself without any guilt, shame or blame - holy, acceptable and well pleasing in His sight.

Now consider the ten virgins Jesus spoke about in Matthew 25; they were all being kept for the coming bridegroom; they all slept during an apparent delay; they all had lamps with them but only half of them had prepared themselves by keeping their lamps full of oil.

To examine yourself means that you have sufficient oil in your lamp. Are you daily living by the power of the Holy Spirit? He is the oil, fuelling you with the Life Jesus has with the Father, setting your whole nature - spirit, soul and body - on fire, like the disciples on the day of Pentecost.

Let's pray: Heavenly Father, fill and flood me to overflowing with the Holy Spirit. May my lamp always stay full of the oil of Your Spirit so I may shine forth the warmth of Your love and Life.

In Jesus' Name, Amen.

Examine yourself as to whether you are in the faith. Test yourselves. Do you not know yourselves, that Jesus Christ is in you? Unless indeed you are disqualified.

2 Corinthians 13:5

How do you examine yourself to see that Christ is in you? How can you be sure you are a Christian?

Ask yourself this question: Do you desire to love God more and more? If you can say yes, then you are like Jesus and His Life is in you!

Jesus taught that those who live in fellowship with the Father have a fountain of His Life-giving Spirit in them. Therefore you need no longer see yourself as falling short of God's glory. Because you know the strength of your fellowship with Him is the Life of Jesus in you, He is your Life-giving fountain; He is your Lifeline to God; He is the author and finisher of your faith, and He is able to keep you from falling and present you faultless in the presence of His glory (Jude 24).

Trust the Holy Spirit to help you in your faith until you come to really believe and know for yourself that the Life Jesus has with the Father is in you and can recognise His Life in you and others.

Like any tree that is deeply rooted in the soil from which it receives its nourishment and strength, so let the roots of your faith grow deep into Jesus Christ Himself.

When the Scripture says, 'Examine yourselves that Christ is in you', automatically deep within your heart you know, 'I have been crucified with Christ; it is no longer I who live but Christ lives in me' (Galatians 2:20).

Oh, let your heart rejoice, dear child of God, that the Life Jesus has with the Father is in you.

His Life in you will perfect you in your fellowship with the Father and you will see the wonderful fruit of His Life as you begin to love yourself as He loves you and learn to love others as you are loved (John 15:9).

Let's pray: Heavenly Father, I love loving You; I love living in fellowship with You; I love who You have made me through Your Life in me; I love loving others as You love me.

In Jesus' Name, Amen.

*According to my earnest expectation and hope that in nothing
I shall be ashamed, but with all boldness, as always, so now also
Christ will be magnified in my body, whether by life or by death*
Philippians 1:20

The gospel of grace is given to unveil the truth of the Life Jesus
has with the Father - a Life that knows no sin, no separation from
the Father's love; it knows no falling short of His glory, no failure,
no shame, no guilt, no condemnation.

So much of Adam's fallen nature (in which we all share) has
shame at its core. This drives you on to all kinds of distorted
images of God, yourself and others. But Jesus Christ - who is the
perfect image of God - has no shame! He came to liberate you
never to suffer this devilish, sinful nature of shame ever again by
giving you His Life.

Oh, let those tears of sorrow turn to joy as the Son of Righteousness
bursts upon your soul and you walk free from the prison of
shame. No more fear of what people think or say about you, but
the sweet confidence of Jesus that God is your Father and you are
living in His favour.

Let me show you the faith of Jesus who loves you.

What a wonderful Heavenly Father we have to give us all the same
faith!

The faith I am talking about is the faith of Jesus. As you can
see in the gospels, Jesus lived in unbroken fellowship with
the Father. He knew by faith that the Father was always with
Him. He knew by faith that the Father always heard Him.
He knew by faith that the Life He lived in the body came from
the Father.

Now you have been given this same faith! You know by faith you are living in unbroken fellowship with the Father. You know by faith He is always with you, He always hears you and enables you to think His thoughts and speak His words and do His works because the Life you now live in the body comes from Him (John 14:12-13).

Oh dear child of God, there is no more pain of shame to hurt you now that you are filled with the Life Jesus has with the Father.

Let's pray: Heavenly Father, I thank You that in nothing I will be ashamed of myself but that in all I am, say and do, the Life Jesus has with You is revealed in me.

In Jesus' Name, Amen.

According to my earnest expectation and hope that in nothing I shall be ashamed, but with all boldness, as always, so now also Christ will be magnified in my body, whether by life or by death

Philippians 1:20

Whether in this life or before the throne of God in heaven, let your earnest expectation be that in nothing you will be ashamed of yourself but that Jesus Christ will be magnified in you (2 Corinthians 5:9-10; Acts 24:16).

Pray and believe that it pleases the Fathers to reveal His Son in you (Galatians 1:16).

Every day, as you arise to your God-given worth and significance in the Lord Jesus Christ, clothe yourself with His Life (Romans 13:14; Galatians 3:27).

As it is written, 'Let him who glories, glory in this: that he understands and knows Me (personally and practically), that I am the Lord, who practices loving-kindness, judgment and righteousness in the earth, for in these things I delight says the Lord' (Jeremiah 9:24 AMPB).

You can be tempted to set your expectations on such unsettling things as man's praise or your own performance, but God has something much better in mind - Christ in you - with His Life in you, you can be sure you will not be disappointed in this life or before His throne.

The Apostle Paul gladly suffered the loss of all things to know Christ in him. He could not see himself receiving any greater honour than that of bearing the image of Jesus.

Now if you cannot see this Life in you or hear His Word, be encouraged for the Holy Spirit is here to help you (1 Corinthians 2:9).

Remember, Jesus promised that when the Holy Spirit comes, 'He will glorify Me, for He will take of what is Mine and declare it to you' (John 16:14).

Now with this in mind be fervent in your love for Jesus, rejoice in Him and trust the Father to reveal the Life Jesus has with Him in you continuously, now and forever.

Let's pray: Heavenly Father, I worship You. I love You Jesus. I lift my hands and lift my voice to praise You with every breath.

In Jesus' Name, Amen.

Now to Him who is able to keep you from stumbling, and to present you faultless before the presence of His glory with exceeding joy

Jude 24

Have you ever thought of going to heaven? Does that seem real to you?! It was real for Enoch, who pleased God so much that he was taken up to heaven (Genesis 5:21-24). It was real for Abraham and Sarah as they desired a better - that is, a heavenly – country (Hebrews 11:16). It was real for Jacob when he saw the angels ascending and descending from heaven (Genesis 28). It was real for Elijah, who went to heaven in a whirlwind (2 Kings 2:11). It was real for King David, who knew he was going there (Psalm 16:9-10; 17:15). Above all it was real for Jesus, who said, 'I go and prepare a place for you' (John 14:3).

Some people want you to think that this earthly life is all there is. But while this life is filled with opportunities for joy and fulfillment, the truth is it is only temporary.

You see Jesus conquered death in order to reveal and to give us eternal Life. When He presented Himself alive to His disciples He said, 'Behold My hands and My feet. Handle Me and see, for a spirit does not have flesh and bones as you see I have' (Luke 24:39). Then He asked them for some food and they gave Him some fish and He ate it in their presence. This and many other signs He gave before He was caught up to heaven.

Oh dear child of God, let your mind be set on the things above, where Jesus is seated at the right hand of God, and not on the things of this earth, for you are no longer of this world because the life you now live is the Life Jesus has with the Father in heaven.

When Jesus returns you will see Him and be caught up with Him to the throne of God to obtain your full inheritance of eternal Life and glory in the presence of the Father.

This hope you have as an anchor for your soul; it is what has given Christians such joy from the day of Jesus' resurrection, that they gladly accepted the loss of all things, knowing they had a better and lasting possession awaiting them in heaven.

Now turn your eyes upon Jesus, look full in His wonderful face, and the things of earth will grow strangely dim in the light of His glory and grace.

Let's pray: Heavenly Father, I trust You to keep me from falling and present me without fault in the presence of Your glory.

In Jesus' Name, Amen.

For we know that if our earthly house, this tent, is destroyed, we have a building from God, a house not made with hands, eternal in the heavens

2 Corinthians 5:1

God was not ashamed to be called the God of Abraham and Sarah because they desired to dwell with Him in a heavenly home and they did this while living by faith in a tent on earth. For God had prepared a city for them of which He was the builder. Their eyes of faith did not grow dim as their earthly tents (this body) began to grow old, but their hope became brighter the nearer they came to departing this world, for they had seen what God had prepared for them a far off, they were assured of it and embraced their future as they confessed they were but strangers and pilgrims on earth (Hebrews 11:13).

Believe God that He is able to give Life to your dying body and keep it for your use in His service until you depart. Do not be dismayed as this earthly tent - your human body – grows old. Trust Him to enlighten the eyes of your heart with the hope set before you so that with joy you can look forward to all God has prepared for you.

King David caught a glimpse of his heavenly home when he said, 'You will show me the path of Life; in Your presence is fullness of joy, at Your right hand are pleasures forevermore' (Psalm 16:11). David also said, 'As for me, I will see Your face in righteousness; I shall be satisfied when I awake in Your likeness' (Psalm 17:15).

Jesus opened the way into this Life. When He was raised from the dead with glorious power, He justified you freely by His grace by giving His Life to dwell in your dying body as a guarantee that you have eternal Life. Now this Life Jesus has with the Father is the priceless gift that awaits you in all its fullness and glory and is perfectly preserved for you in heaven, beyond the reach of death and decay. God Himself in His mighty power will make sure you will get there safely to receive it because you trust Him.

Eternal Life will be yours for all to see as you will be clothed in a heavenly body that knows none of the earthly sorrows of sin and death.

So take courage in this wonderful joy set before you!

Let's pray: Heavenly Father, You have filled my heart with faith that I have eternal Life through Jesus Christ. How I long to live in Your presence forever and ever.

In Jesus' Name, Amen.

But many who are first will be last, and the last first
Matthew 19:30

We know Jesus is exalted to the right hand of God. He is first in everything! However, we need to remember that before this could happen He also gave up His glory as God and was pleased to become like us. Born of a woman and found in the appearance of a man, He did not seek to be served but to serve. In Him we see perfectly the beauty of His Life with the Father as He humbled himself and was willing to demonstrate the Father's love in His obedience unto death, even death on the cross. Therefore He was highly exalted and given the name above every other name, that at the name of Jesus every knee should bow of those in heaven, on earth and under the earth and every tongue should confess that Jesus Christ is Lord to the glory of God!

There is a great lesson for us here: that He who was the highest, the Creator and Maker of all things willingly became the least. Jesus took the lowest place and became poor in suffering our shame of sin in death in order to make us rich in the Life of His exaltation and glory at the throne of God.

This is why the love of Jesus compels you to deny yourself and, like Him, love others as you lay down your life to serve them. For he who seeks to exalt himself will be humbled - humbled by the lower nature of pride, fear, anger and all sorts of torment. But he who humbles himself will lay down his life in love and be exalted with the loving Life of Jesus.

Moses stands out in history as one of the greatest men who has ever lived. Yet God declared that he was the humblest man on earth (Numbers 12:3). Moses became the least of men in bearing the burden of God and His people, giving his life to lead them to the Promised Land. However in glory, he was seen among the first to represent God and His holy law as he bore witness on the Mount of Transfiguration that Jesus is the Christ.

May this grace of the humility of Jesus Christ find deep roots in your character so that it pleases the Father to see His Son in you and so that you may be among the first in heaven.

Let's pray: Heavenly Father, I know You love me because You grant me to share the Life Jesus has with You in heaven. How I long for the humble servant's heart of Jesus to be revealed in me.
In Jesus' Name, Amen.

Most assuredly, I say to you, a servant is not greater than his master; nor is he who is sent greater than he who sent him
John 13:16

You can clearly see the Life Jesus has with the Father when He humbly served His disciples by washing their feet.

Jesus said, 'If I, your Lord and Teacher, have washed your feet, you also ought to wash one another's feet. If you know these things, blessed are you if you do them' (John 13:14-17).

God's blessings flow from those who, like Jesus, know the Father's love. This Life in the Father's love is seen as Jesus gave Himself not just to wash His disciple's feet but all our sins in His own precious blood.

How Jesus longed for His disciples to see and experience this grace of His Life in the Father's love and take it to the whole world.

However, when the disciples saw the glory Jesus has with the Father through His compassion, healing the multitudes, they said, 'Lord, grant us to rule with You.' Jesus had to show them that this glory does not come to those who seek to rule but only to those who take up their cross, deny themselves and lay down their lives to serve those around them.

You see, the servant heart of Jesus lies at the root of all greatness in God. Jesus said, 'Whoever desires to become great among you shall be your servant. And whoever of you desires to be first shall be slave of all. For even the Son of Man did not come to be served, but to serve and to give His life a ransom for many' (Mark 10:43-45).

I pray that the revelation of the Life Jesus has with the Father fills your heart so you may know for yourself through experience this compelling force of God's love that enables you to have the servant heart of Jesus!

Jesus will open the river of His heavenly Life in the Father's love through you to bless all those around you as you sweetly lay down your life to serve them.

Let's pray: Heavenly Father, help me to know this grace of the servant heart of Jesus in me so I can see the river of Your blessings flow through me.

In Jesus' Name, Amen.

For even the Son of Man did not come to be served, but to serve, and to give His life a ransom for many

Mark 10:45

As you learn from Jesus to love others, you will discover the privilege of bearing their burdens, empowering them with His Life and so fulfilling the law of Christ (Galatians 6:2).

When Jesus bore the burden of your weak human nature on the cross He did not become angry or offended but was full of grace and truth. The grace that poured out of Him revealed the truth of a Life that knows no sin - a Life that gives light to every man to know that God is love.

This Life of Jesus enables you to absorb human failings and not make anyone feel guilty or condemned but instead forgiven, loved and empowered.

This is God's great mandate for you, that with the grace and ability of Jesus you serve others by taking no account or making a record of a suffered wrong, but by gladly forbearing them in love without giving up.

You see, it is an honour for a man of understanding to overlook a transgression, for he who covers and forgives seeks love (Proverbs 19:11; 17:9).

You may say, yes, but shouldn't people apologise? Not if you do not make a charge against them! Jesus will give you His power to minister His reconciliation by enabling you not to impute their trespasses and make a charge against them in your heart. In this you start to manifest the Life of Jesus that is in you. As it is written, 'He has not punished us as we deserve for all our sins. He has removed our sins as far away from us as the east is from the west. He is like a Father to us tender and sympathetic' (Psalm 103:10-12 LB). This is the grace of God - Jesus paid it all. He has cleared your record; there is no charge!

You may say, 'Yes, I want to be a source of His grace. I want to serve others in His love and bear their burdens, but what about those things that must change?'

Dear child of God, was it not the Spirit of Life in Jesus that set you free?

Will not this same Spirit of Life that now lives in you - the Life Jesus has with the Father - set others free too?

Let's pray: Heavenly Father, fill me with Your grace; enable me to absorb another's failings; help me not to get angry or offended, nor to make anyone feel guilty or condemned. Equip me to love and empower others.

In Jesus' Name, Amen.

For even the Son of Man did not come to be served, but to serve, and to give His life a ransom for many.

Mark 10:45

It pleased God to anoint Jesus with the Holy Spirit and power as He went about moved with compassion, doing good, healing all who were oppressed by the devil (Acts 10:38).

How beautiful to see a completely unselfish person filled with love, serving others!

This is something the sinful soul cannot understand because the sinful, selfish nature suffers anger and offence and always needs to be served or end up being separated from others. But the sinless Life Jesus lived on earth was a heavenly Life in that He came not to be served but to serve and give His Life for many. Oh, how the Heavenly Father longs for this same unselfish, self-sacrificing love of Jesus to flow through you.

You see, Jesus was a man of sorrows - that means pain not anger. When He suffered the pain of our human nature, grace and healing began to flow from His heart. Now this same grace and healing He gives to flow from you as you learn from Him to feel pain instead of anger and experience His grace instead of offence.

You may say, but what do I do when I cannot withstand the temptation to become angry and offended? Don't get stuck in the thought that you were provoked and it is not your fault. Take responsibility for your own behavior; don't excuse yourself by accusing. Be humble. Ask for forgiveness! And don't feel a failure when you fail to show grace. Remember Jesus said, 'My grace is sufficient for you for my strength is made perfect in weakness' (2 Corinthians 12:9). You are not a failure! You are a learner, learning to know the grace of Jesus in you.

Don't give up! Jesus believes in you! He will give you, out of the rich treasury of His Life with the Father, all you need for doing the same works He does.

Oh, how it pleases the Father to see you anointed with the Holy Spirit, moved with His compassion, going about your daily life doing good, loving and healing precious people.

Let's pray: Heavenly Father, I know it pleases You to see me anointed with the Holy Spirit and with power so that I may serve and give my life to love others like Jesus.

In Jesus' Name, Amen.

Then Jesus said to His disciples, 'If anyone desires to come after Me, let him deny himself, and take up his cross, and follow Me'
Matthew 16:24

The servant heart of Jesus is one of the great trademarks of all who bear His Spirit.

Jesus told everyone who followed Him to deny themselves and take up their cross. 'For to this you were called, because Christ also suffered for us, leaving us an example, that you should follow His steps, who committed no sin, nor was deceit found in His mouth, who, when He was reviled, did not revile in return; when He suffered, He did not threaten, but committed Himself to Him who judges righteously; who Himself bore our sins in His own body on the tree, that we, having died to sins, might live for righteousness, by whose stripes you were healed' (1 Peter 2:21-24).

To deny yourself and take up your cross is to take the sins of others, absorb them like a sponge, and let them die and become powerless in you. While this can cause pain, as it did for Jesus, you will experience His Spirit of grace.

You see, to follow Jesus is to do what He did - to take away the sins of others and release them from every charge. This grace of God to take away sin is one of the sweetest of all the graces of His great love.

I understand that some sins are exceedingly sorrowful and cause much pain, but remember, where sin abounded grace abounded much more (Romans 5:20). Believe that even as the Father out of the rich treasury of His glory gave Jesus the power to take away sin, so He empowers you to do the same (Matthew 9:6; 2 Corinthians 5:18-21).

Remember when the kindness and love of God our Saviour toward man appeared; it was not by any good we had done, but according to His mercy that He saved us, through the washing of regeneration and renewing of the Holy Spirit, whom He poured out on us abundantly through Jesus, justifying us freely by His grace (Titus 3:4-7). Now believe this same kindness and love of God our Saviour is in you!

Begin to sing, 'There is a fountain filled with blood, drawn from Emmanuel's veins, And sinners plunged beneath that flood lose all their guilty stains, lose all their guilty stains, lose all their guilty stains, And sinners plunged beneath that flood lose all their guilty stains.'

Let's pray: Heavenly Father, grant me to know and grow in this grace to deny myself, to take up my cross and take away sin through Your kindness and love.

In Jesus' Name, Amen.

There is a fountain filled with blood drawn
from Emmanuel's veins;
And sinners plunged beneath that flood lose all their guilty stains.
Lose all their guilty stains, lose all their guilty stains;
And sinners plunged beneath that flood lose all their guilty stains.

The dying thief rejoiced to see that fountain in his day;
And there have I, though vile as he, washed all my sins away.
Washed all my sins away, washed all my sins away;
And there have I, though vile as he, washed all my sins away.

Dear dying Lamb, Thy precious blood shall never lose its power
Till all the ransomed church of God be saved, to sin no more.
Be saved, to sin no more, be saved, to sin no more;
Till all the ransomed church of God be saved, to sin no more.

E'er since, by faith, I saw the stream Thy flowing wounds supply,
Redeeming love has been my theme, and shall be till I die.
And shall be till I die, and shall be till I die;
Redeeming love has been my theme, and shall be till I die.

Then in a nobler, sweeter song, I'll sing Thy power to save,
When this poor lisping, stammering tongue lies silent in the grave.
Lies silent in the grave, lies silent in the grave;
When this poor lisping, stammering tongue lies silent in the grave.

Lord, I believe Thou hast prepared, unworthy though I be,
For me a blood bought free reward, a golden harp for me!
'Tis strung and tuned for endless years,
and formed by power divine,
To sound in God the Father's ears no other name but Thine.

William Cowper, 1772.

As the Father loved Me, I also have loved you; abide in My love
John 15:9

What is the secret to this grace that has the power to take away sin? Where does this grace come from? It comes from the heart of our God and Saviour Jesus Christ who bore the sins of all mankind. As it is written, 'He endured the suffering that should have been ours, the pain that we should have borne. All the while we thought that His suffering was punishment sent by God. But because of our sins He was wounded, beaten because of the evil we did. We are healed by the punishment He suffered, made whole by the blows He received' (Isaiah 53:4-5 TEV).

You see Jesus was made manifest to take away your sins, for in Him there is no sin. This means Jesus never failed to reveal the Life He has with the Father (1 John 3:5). So when Jesus says, 'Abide in My love, even as I abide in My Father's love', He is showing you the way into this grace that breaks the power of sin and sets the captive free. All you have to do is abide in His love and your heart will be filled with His grace.

These are some of the qualities of His grace you will find as you abide in His love: His love will enable you to be tender-hearted, peace-loving, courteous, patient and kind; it will enable you to allow for discussion and be willing to yield, never to envy, or to be proud or rude. This love is the mercy and goodness of God and will always compel you to be wholehearted, straightforward and sincere. When you abide in His love and suffer the weaknesses of others, you will feel pain instead of anger, compassion instead of condemnation, intercession instead of judgment, and for you it will be an honour to overlook a fault, clear the record and have no charge.

You see Christ's love will compel you to do something good no matter how dim things may seem – to always believe the best and never give up.

Now when the pain of what others say or do begins to break you down, you know what is the priority for you - spend more time abiding in His love so that a fresh supply of His boundless love and kindness may flood your soul and make you whole. As you learn to abide in His love and partake of His grace, you come to realise that you cannot let yourself be drawn out of His love because if you do, the cost is great to your own soul, not to mention the sorrow you may cause another.

Again I charge you in mercy to let nothing draw you out of His great love so that His grace may never stop flowing from your heart.

Let's pray: Heavenly Father, You said nothing can separate me from the love I have in Jesus. Father, teach me to abide in Your love like Jesus so that this river of Your grace may never stop flowing from my heart.

In Jesus' Name, Amen.

And I have declared to them Your name, and will declare it, that
the love with which You loved Me may be in them, and I in them
John 17:26

What is the secret to abiding in the Father's love?

For Jesus, abiding in the love of the Father meant that He desired that the Father be glorified in and through His life. Jesus did not seek His own glory; He sought the Father's glory. It is the sin nature which makes you think separate from God for it seeks its own glory. But Jesus never sinned; He stayed perfectly one with the Father.

Remember when Jesus was in the upper room on the night He was betrayed, He shared about His body being a sacrifice for sin and about the new covenant in His blood. Then, when Judas left the room to betray Him, Jesus said, 'Now the Son of Man is glorified, and God is glorified in Him. If God is glorified in Him, God will also glorify Him in Himself, and glorify Him immediately' (John 13:31-32).

Jesus believed that the Father would receive great glory through His suffering, death and resurrection. He believed that when the Father was glorified in Him, He would share in His glory.

Dear child of God, let this also be your heart's desire - to abide in His love and share His glory. For the love of Christ will compel you to love others as He loves you so that the Father will receive great glory by what He will be able to accomplish through you.

Jesus prayed, 'Father, I gave them the glory You gave Me, the glory of being one with You, I in them even as You are in Me so the world will know You sent Me and have loved them as much as You have loved Me' (John 17:22-23 LB).

Now what more can you ask for than to share the glory of God.

Pray, 'Not unto us, O Lord, not unto us, but to Your name give glory, because of Your mercy, because of Your truth' (Psalm 115:1).

'To God be the glory' is the simple secret to abiding in His love!

Let's pray: Heavenly Father, I know You love me! How I long to abide in Your love and stay one with You. I do not seek my own glory but long for You to be glorified in me.

In Jesus' Name, Amen.

Having disarmed principalities and powers, He made a public spectacle of them, triumphing over them in it

Colossians 2:15

Give glory to God by letting the life you live and the love you give stand in reference to the accomplished work of Jesus.

Jesus suffered and died on the cross to pay the penalty for the sins of all men, forever. Therefore never let Satan use the shortcomings and weaknesses of others to employ you to do his evil work of accusing the brethren (Revelation 12:10-11).

When you take those strong demonic feelings of offence and accusation and absorb them like a sponge, letting them die in you, they become powerless and of no effect. When you refuse to give authority to such feelings by speaking them out you are disarming the devil, you are making a spectacle of him and triumphing over him, just as Jesus did.

This is what it means to suffer with Jesus, for when you feel the pain of another's offences, as Jesus did all of ours, you are suffering together with Him (Philippians 3:10). And when you do this and you pray, like Jesus, 'Father forgive them,' His Spirit of grace is in you. Now when His Spirit of grace is in you, you will know and experience that Jesus reigns over all sin and all the power of the enemy. His Spirit of grace not only lets sin die in you and thereby disarms Satan, but also enables you to impart the Life Jesus has with the Father.

Oh, how immeasurable is the width and the length, the depth and the height of the love of Jesus! This, dear child of God, is the grace by which He employs you to absorb the offences of others and to let them die in you, enabling you to take no account of a suffered wrong and to remove every charge, disarming the enemy and, most wonderful of all, imparting the Life Jesus has with the Father that knows no condemnation.

Now make the Lord Jesus happy by the life you live and the love you give; love your enemies, bless those who curse you, do good to those who hate you, and pray for those who spitefully use you and persecute you, so that like Jesus you may be beloved sons and daughters of your Father in heaven (Matthew 5:44-46).

Let's pray: Heavenly Father, I long to give You glory. I pray the life I live and the love I give stands in reference to the accomplished work of Jesus on the cross. I thank You for enabling me to absorb, disarm and empower.

In Jesus' Name, Amen.

And I have declared to them Your name, and will declare it, that
the love with which You loved Me may be in them, and I in them
John 17:26

There is only so much you can do in your own strength even if
you are a most generous person. But look at Jesus who went
beyond all human limitations to demonstrate God's love while
we were yet sinners. This same love that enabled Him is now
being poured into your heart by the Holy Spirit so that you can
love as He loves.

God would have you live in such a grace where His abilities
become your ability.

Sure there are moments when you will feel so very human and
limited that you may say, 'I can do nothing.'

But when you feel powerless, don't despair, for as you make
known to God your needs and trust Him for the answers, He
Himself will move in you with His love to bring about the
answers.

You see this moving of God's love in you is what the Bible calls
compassion, and compassion causes the natural to become subject
to the supernatural.

Jesus said that He could do nothing if He were not moved by
God's love.

He lived in His love and from it He was able to do the impossible
(John 5:19).

So with the Holy Spirit's help, follow God's example in everything
you do, just as a much loved child imitates his father.

Be full of love and compassion, be tender-hearted, gracious and kind, be courteous, friendly and polite, following the example of Jesus who loves you and gave Himself for you.

His love never fails!

Now live and love out of the vast resources of the Life Jesus has with the Father in you.

Let's pray: Heavenly Father, I embrace Your love! Thank You Holy Spirit, for filling me with the Father's love so that I can love others with His love.

In Jesus' Name, Amen.

And I have declared to them Your name, and will declare it, that
the love with which You loved Me may be in them, and I in them
John 17:26

It will far surpass your highest hopes and dreams to discover you are loved as much as Jesus, especially when you see the intimacy He shares with the Father.

Dearly beloved, the Holy Spirit is in you to reveal the Life Jesus has with the Father. He will daily renew you in your mind and open the Scriptures to you to show you all Jesus has done for you.

Think about this, Jesus has made you one with the Father through His precious blood - washing, cleansing, regenerating and renewing your heart and mind, setting you free from consciousness of sin so you may know by experience for yourself the wonderful Life He has with the Father.

Oh, how God longs for you to believe Him when He tells you that He loves you dearly, so that you may feel His warm love flowing through you.

God is love, and anyone who lives in love is living in God and God is living in him (1 John 4:16).

This is the work of His grace, Jesus is drawing you up into the Life He has with the Father to perfect the way you think, so that you may know, no matter what happens, you are loved by the Father.

I am convinced that nothing can ever separate you from His love.

Neither life nor death can separate you. The angels would never do that and all the powers of hell cannot keep God's love away from you.

Fears for today or worries about tomorrow cannot separate you from His love.

If you are high in the sky or deep in the deepest ocean, nothing will ever be able to separate you from the love of God which Jesus so generously and continuously pours into your heart through the Life He has with the Father (Romans 8:37-39 LB).

Let's pray: Heavenly Father, I know and believe that the love You have for me is the same love You have for Jesus. You are so good to me! I know and believe that nothing can separate me from Your love.

In Jesus' Name, Amen.

And I have declared to them Your name, and will declare it, that
the love with which You loved Me may be in them, and I in them
John 17:26

Can you see the greatness of the love with which the Father loves Jesus? It is immeasurable and everlasting.

Jesus spoke about the Father's love for Him all the time. He said, 'I can do nothing but the Father loves Me and shows Me all things.' (John 5:19) 'He who loves Me will be loved by My Father' (John 14:21). You see, Jesus knows the love of the Father and longs for you to know this love too. This is why Jesus prayed 'that they all may be one, as You, Father, are in Me, and I in You; that they also may be one in us, that the love with which You loved Me may be in them and I in them' (John 17:21, 26). Oh, the glory of the fullness of the Life Jesus has with the Father! To be loved like Him is beyond what we can comprehend without seeing it in Him.

Think about this, the Father loves Jesus so much He revealed all of Himself in Him (Colossians 1:19) and appointed Him to sit at His right hand. In His own righteousness God was able to reveal in Jesus His own eternal holiness, His light of Life, His character, His goodness, His loving-kindness, His faithfulness - yes, the fullness of Himself. This Life Jesus has in the love of the Father is what He now communicates to you, and being seated at His throne means Jesus has all the power to draw you up into this Life.

Consider the Apostle Paul, and be encouraged in believing and knowing God loves you!

Paul said, 'I used to scoff at the name of Jesus. I hunted down His people, harming them in every way I could. God had mercy on me because I didn't know what I was doing, for I didn't know Jesus at that time. Oh, how kind the Lord Jesus was, for He showed me how to trust Him and become full of His love. How true it is, and how I long that everyone should know it, that Jesus came into the world to save sinners and I was the greatest of them all. But God had mercy on me so that Jesus could use me as an example to show you how patient He is with even the worst sinners, so that you will realise that you, too, can have everlasting life.' (1 Timothy 1:13-17 NLT).

Let's pray: Heavenly Father, You love me like You love Jesus. How wonderful Your love is to me! I am quiet and at rest before You because I know You love me.

In Jesus' Name, Amen.

We love because God first loved us

1 John 4:19 (TEV)

What wonder and glory when the love of the Father is poured into your heart by the Holy Spirit and you are able to love like Jesus. You see, the love of Jesus was like sweet perfume to the Father. This is why His blood is so powerful because it has no condemnation but only the loving intercession of a Saviour, crying, 'Father, forgive them!'

Now believe God to enable you to love like Jesus. Trust the Holy Spirit to perfect His love in you so that when you bleed (and I do not mean literally but emotionally) there will be no condemnation or evil flowing from your heart but only the sweet love of Jesus.

Jesus said, 'Love your enemies, do good to those who hate you, bless those who curse you, and pray for those who spitefully use you. To those who strike you on the cheek, offer the other also' (Luke 6:27-29).

'Speak evil of no one but be peaceful and friendly, and always show a gentle attitude toward everyone' (Titus 3:2 TEV). 'Bless and do not curse' (Romans 12:14).

'Let no foul or polluting language, nor evil word nor unwholesome or worthless talk ever come out of your mouth, but only such speech as is good and beneficial to the spiritual progress of others, as is fitting to the need and the occasion, that it may be a blessing and give grace and favour to those who hear you. Do not grieve the Holy Spirit of God. Let all bitterness and indignation and wrath (passion, rage, bad temper) and resentment (anger, animosity) and quarrelling (brawling, clamour, contention) and slander (evil-speaking, abusive or blasphemous language) be banished from you, with all malice (spite, ill will, or baseness of any kind). Become useful and helpful and kind to one another, tender-hearted (compassionate, understanding, loving-hearted), forgiving one another readily and freely, as God in Christ forgave you' (Ephesians 4:29-5:1 AMPB).

Dear child of God, the Father will pour His love into your heart by the Holy Spirit.

He will enable you to love others with His love.

Let's pray: Heavenly Father, teach me to love like Jesus. I want to learn from You how to love others.

In Jesus' Name, Amen.

But I know you, that you do not have the love of God in you
John 5:42

How can you know you have the love of God in you?

Jesus told those who heard Him that if they received Him the love of God was in them.

The reason this was so important was because people had embraced a culture of rejection under which many suffered, so much so that even Jesus, who represented the love of the Father, was rejected. Rejecting Jesus showed that people did not have God's love in them. But those who did receive Jesus showed that they did have God's love in them.

Jesus said, 'Your disapproval means nothing to Me because I know you don't have the love of God in you, for I have come to you representing My Father and you refuse to welcome Me, though you readily enough receive those who aren't sent from Him, but represent only themselves! No wonder you can't believe I came from My Father because you don't care what He thinks about Me' (John 5:41-44).

But 'He who loves Me will be loved by My Father, and I will love him and manifest Myself to him' (John 14:21).

You know the love of God is in you because your heart burns with love for Jesus and because you are compelled to no longer live for yourself but for Him who loves you and gave Himself for you and to love others as much as He loves you.

Perhaps the above title startled you.

Can it be you do not have the love of God in you? Well ask yourself, do you see others the way Jesus does or is your heart dark with evil thoughts? Are you suspicious, judging others? Do you easily become entangled with gossip? Do you quickly see what is wrong with others and even think this is a gift of God? Then you don't know Jesus!

Jesus did not demonstrate God's love this way - just the opposite. He saw people the way God saw them, no matter what was wrong with them, and it was His love for them that began to restore them.

Let's pray: Heavenly Father, I open my heart to Your love. Set me on fire with Your love and help me to see others the way You see them.

In Jesus' Name, Amen.

*Therefore, from now on, we regard no one according to the
flesh. Even though we have known Christ according to the flesh,
yet now we know Him thus no longer*

2 Corinthians 5:16

Jesus expected His disciples to recognise God in Him when He
said, 'He who has seen Me has seen the Father.' Jesus also expects
you to have this same ability when He said, 'You will know I am
in the Father, and you are in Me, and I in you' (John 14:9, 20).

Remember when Jesus asked His disciples, 'Who do you say
I am?' Peter replied, 'You are the Christ, the Son of the living
God.' Jesus said to Peter, 'My Father has revealed this to you.'

This shows that God Himself will teach you how to recognise the
Life Jesus has with Him in yourself and others.

For to know someone after their natural nature is earthly, but to
recognise the Life of Jesus in someone is heavenly!

When you think someone is a Christian what do you see?

Oh, how the Father longs for you to recognise those who are born
of Him for He desires to open your eyes and show you how much
He loves His children.

This is the great heart of the Father's love for you, not only to
reveal Jesus in you, but to empower you to recognise Him in
others so you can love them with His love.

The great commandment of Jesus to love others as He loves you
is not a burden but an opportunity for you to experience the love
of the Father.

For nothing is more wonderful than to love others with the love of the Father.

Let's pray: Heavenly Father, teach me and empower me to recognise the Life Jesus has with You in myself and others. I want to learn to love as You love.

In Jesus' Name, Amen.

And you also became God's people when you heard the true message, the Good News that brought you salvation. You believed in Christ, and God put His stamp of ownership on you by giving you the Holy Spirit He had promised

Ephesians 1:13 (TEV)

Those who are unspiritual and legalistic have sought to identify who God's people are. However, their perspective is limited since God only reveals such things through His Spirit.

Those who don't have the Holy Spirit do not understand the things of the Spirit, but all who have the Holy Spirit learn from the Spirit to see things God's way (1 Corinthians 2:9-10).

Jesus said, 'John the Baptist was a burning shining light because he bore witness of the truth.' John bore witness of Jesus, saying, 'I saw the Spirit descending from heaven like a dove, and He remained upon Him. I did not know Him, but He who sent me to baptise with water said to me, 'Upon whom you see the Spirit descending, and remaining on Him, this is He who baptises with the Holy Spirit.' And I have seen and testified that this is the Son of God' (John 1:32-34).

You see, it was God Himself who taught John to recognise Jesus by seeing the Holy Spirit's seal on Him, and God was pleased that John believed what He showed him.

'Now all of you who heard the Good News how to be saved and trusted in Jesus were marked as belonging to Him by the Holy Spirit who long ago had been promised to all of us Christians. His presence within you is God's guarantee that He will give you all He has promised and the Spirit's seal upon you means that God has already purchased you and guarantees to bring you to Himself' (Ephesians 1:13-14 LB).

When the Apostle Peter was learning this he said, 'God has shown me in a vision that I should never think of anyone as inferior' (Acts 10:28; Galatians 3:26-29).

I pray these words will deeply penetrate your heart, so that like Peter you can learn to recognise those God has given His Spirit and love them with His love.

Let's pray: Heavenly Father, I believe what You say and trust You to teach me to recognise Your Spirit's seal on others and to love them as You love me.

In Jesus' Name, Amen.

And because of what Christ did, all you others too, who heard the Good News about how to be saved, and trusted Christ, were marked as belonging to Christ by the Holy Spirit, who long ago had been promised to all of us Christians

Ephesians 1:13 (LB)

What joy beyond comprehension that God Himself has marked you as His own, by giving you the Holy Spirit!

What more evidence do you need that you are well-pleasing to Him?

When God the Father gave the Holy Spirit to Jesus He said, 'You are my beloved Son; in You I am well pleased' (Luke.3:22).

By giving you the Holy Spirit, God is saying to you, 'You are My beloved child; in you I am well pleased!'

So let your heart find rest in His great love and be fully convinced that you have been accepted in the Beloved (Ephesians 1:6).

The mark you bear of the indwelling presence and power of the Holy Spirit is like the glory of God shining from the face of Moses. While the glory on Moses would fade, it will only grow brighter and brighter in you until the day you see Jesus (Proverbs 4:18; 1Thessalonians 1:10).

Do not fear, dear child of God, that the light of Christ's Life in you will ever fade away!

Remember, the great ministry of Jesus at the throne of God is to maintain His glorious Life in you.

Jesus said, 'The Holy Spirit will abide with you forever' (John 14:16; Isaiah 59:21).

The Holy Spirit in you is the light of the Life which was shining from Moses' face and which also set Jesus ablaze on the Mount of Transfiguration. To His great delight this same Holy Spirit is now also living in you as a down payment of the glory that awaits you.

So look at the joy set before you and bear the mark of the Holy Spirit, to the praise of the glory of God's grace, until you see Him face to face.

Let's pray: Heavenly Father, I worship You in Spirit and truth for I know You are my Father and like Jesus I am Your child, marked by Your Spirit.

In Jesus' Name, Amen.

The Spirit is God's guarantee that He will give us the inheritance He promised and that He has purchased us to be His own people. He did this so we would praise and glorify Him

Ephesians 1:14 (NLT)

Because you believe Jesus is the Christ, the Son of the living God, you are given the Holy Spirit as the guarantee that you have eternal Life. The Holy Spirit you have received is the same power that raised Jesus from the dead (Ephesians 1:19-20)! This is why you have all the assurance you need to believe you are saved.

The Scripture says, 'Whoever believes on Him will not be put to shame.' 'Whoever calls on the name of the Lord shall be saved' (Romans 10:11, 13).

Jesus said, 'He who believes in the Son has everlasting Life' (John 3:36).

And now the Holy Spirit in you also bears witness with your spirit that God is your Father by enabling you to worship Him in Spirit and truth as you cry, 'Abba, Father!' (Romans 8:15-16).

This seal of ownership God has placed on you is no less powerful than what was given to Jesus.

Now dear child of God, be forever persuaded and convinced, no matter how humanly weak you may feel or how much Satan may challenge you, that God is your Father and you are His child!

The seal of the Holy Spirit is an unbreakable bond between you and the Father because the Father in His divine providence has given Jesus who is the very embodiment of eternal Life – the new creation – to sit at His right hand. This is so that God Himself can uphold you with His Life while you are still in your earthly body and guarantee that this Life is kept safe for you to receive in all its fullness as the reward of your faith in Jesus when you appear before Him (1 Peter 1:3-5).

Rejoice therefore in the Lord Jesus and again I say rejoice in Jesus. He is a mighty Saviour. He will not fail you. He will never leave you, so trust Him!

Let's pray: Heavenly Father, I believe Jesus is Your Son, living in me. I believe I have eternal Life for I bear Your seal of ownership, the Holy Spirit, whom You said will abide with me and in me forever.

In Jesus' Name, Amen.

For we know that when this earthly tent we live in is taken down (that is, when we die and leave this earthly body), we will have a house in heaven, an eternal body made for us by God Himself and not by human hands. We grow weary in our present bodies, and we long to put on our heavenly bodies like new clothing. For we will put on heavenly bodies; we will not be spirits without bodies. While we live in these earthly bodies, we groan and sigh, but it's not that we want to die and get rid of these bodies that clothe us. Rather, we want to put on our new bodies so that these dying bodies will be swallowed up by life. God Himself has prepared us for this, and as a guarantee He has given us His Holy Spirit

2 Corinthians 5:1-5 (NLT)

Remember when Jesus was in prayer on the Mount of Transfiguration how He was transformed with the glory of the Life He has with the Father. His face shone like the sun and His clothes became as white as the light (Matthew 17:2).

Jesus prayed, 'Father, I desire that they also whom You gave Me may be with Me where I am, that they may behold My glory which You have given Me; for You loved Me before the foundation of the world' (John 17:24).

This is your glorious inheritance ready to be revealed at the appearing of Jesus when He will be glorified in you. On that Day He will be admired in the glory reflected in you who believe in Him (2 Thessalonians 1:10 AMPB).

When you see Jesus, in the twinkling of an eye, you will enter the fullness of your inheritance and be just like Him. For He who subdues all things to Himself by the greatness of the power of His glory will clothe you with your eternal heavenly body so that for the joy of His accomplished work He may present you to the Father - holy and without blame, glorious in His sight.

Having this hope while you are still in your earthly body, do not look at the things that can be seen, which are temporal, but fix your attention on the things above, where Jesus is seated at the right hand of God. For you know by faith according to what is written and through the Holy Spirit in you, that the Life you now bear in this earthen vessel of your natural body is the Life Jesus has with the Father, and this Life will soon be unveiled in all its glory at the appearing of Jesus.

Praise God for Jesus who is your Life!

Let's pray: Heavenly Father, Your blessings are without measure for the Life You have given Jesus is in me. I long to see Jesus and be just like Him.

In Jesus' Name, Amen.

For though I might desire to boast, I will not be a fool; for I will speak the truth. But I refrain, lest anyone should think of me above what he sees me to be or hears from me
                                                            2 Corinthians 12:6

Under certain circumstances it can be anyone's temptation to boast, and while this can seem harmless and even amusing, the closer you live in fellowship with the Father the less attractive this becomes as you are filled with the truth of His Life and cannot bear to misrepresent Him.

Again, while boasting may seem harmless it can become a stumbling block in our lives to prevent us from representing the truth of the Life we have with the Father.

Dear child of God, we can clearly see in Jesus that He never misrepresented the Father or made any claims that were beneath or beyond the measure of the Life He had with Him.

When Jesus said, 'I am the resurrection and the Life,' He was talking about where He lived in God - something He confirmed not just in raising Lazarus (who had been dead for four days) but in His own resurrection on the third day, as God foretold in Scripture.

In your life too, God will fill your heart and mind with His thoughts to enable you to speak His word and do His works so that you may have the immeasurable privilege to represent Him in all you are, say and do.

While the Apostle Paul had some heavenly experiences, he did not feel compelled to use them as an advertisement to advance himself but like Jesus he only longed for what the Father worked in Him as a gift to others (2 Corinthians 12:5-6).

Dear child of God, the love of Jesus will compel you never to seek to live beneath or beyond the measure of the Life you have with the Father. This Life He will never fail to reveal in you as you long to represent Him and not yourself.

Let's pray: Heavenly Father, not unto us, O Lord, not unto us, but to Your name give glory, because of Your mercy, because of Your truth. Father I so long for You to be glorified in all I am, say and do.

In Jesus' Name, Amen.

[That you may really come] to know [practically, through experience for yourselves] the love of Christ, which far surpasses mere knowledge [without experience]; that you may be filled [through all your being] unto all the fullness of God [may have the richest measure of the divine Presence, and become a body wholly filled and flooded with God Himself]!

Ephesians 3:19 (AMPB)

What is your expectation of the Christian life while you are still living in your earthly body?

Jesus compels you through His great love to apprehend the joy of becoming a body wholly filled and flooded with God Himself. For God purchased your body with the precious blood of Jesus to be the temple of the Holy Spirit. As it is written, 'For you were bought at a price; therefore glorify God in your body and in your spirit, which are God's' (1 Corinthians 6:20).

This is the Life Jesus lived on earth. As it is written 'And the Word (Christ) became flesh (human, incarnate) and tabernacled (fixed His tent of flesh, lived awhile) among us; and we [actually] saw His glory (His honour, His majesty), such glory as an only begotten Son receives from His Father, full of grace (favour, lovingkindness) and truth' (John 1:14 AMPB).

What greater joy could you live for in your earthly body?

Jesus said, 'You will receive power when the Holy Spirit has come upon you and you will be witnesses unto Me' (Acts 1.8).

Like a consuming fire the Holy Spirit will burn up every feeling of inadequacy so you will no longer feel self-conscious but become Christ-conscious and gladly bear witness of Him.

Multitudes of people who live in darkness and don't know God will see His glory in you and be saved as you share about His love.

Now consider the greatness of the love Jesus has for you that He is drawing you up into the Life He has with the Father so you may live like Him and have the richest measure of the divine presence and become a body wholly filled and flooded with God Himself.

Let's pray: Heavenly Father, I believe my body belongs to Christ and is the temple of the Holy Spirit. How I long to be filled continuously with the richest measure of Your divine presence!

In Jesus' Name, Amen.

Now to Him who, by (in consequence of) the [action of His] power that is at work within us, is able to [carry out His purpose and] do superabundantly, far over and above all that we [dare] ask or think [infinitely beyond our highest prayers, desires, thoughts, hopes, or dreams

Ephesians 3:20 (AMPB)

Jesus rejoiced when He saw His disciples share His glory as they began doing the same works He did (Luke 10:21).

But you can also see that Jesus had sorrow when His disciples were slow to believe they were able to do what He did. Jesus said to His disciples, 'Oh, what tiny faith you have; how much longer must I be with you until you believe? How much longer must I be patient with you?' (Mark 9:19 LB).

You see, you will be able to do the same works Jesus does by accepting every good thing that is in you because of Him (Philemon 1:6).

When Peter learned to live by the power that was at work in him he said, 'What I have I give you; in the name of Jesus Christ of Nazareth, rise up and walk.' And immediately the man who had been lame from his mother's womb leaped up, stood and walked, praising God to the amazement of all.

Now Jesus is calling you, saying, 'Most assuredly, I say to you, believe in Me and the works I do you will do also; and greater works than these you will do, because I go to My Father. Whatever you ask in My name, that I will do, that the Father may be glorified in the Son. If you ask anything in My name, I will do it' (John 14:12-14).

Now, make the Lord Jesus truly happy and be willing to work hard. As the Apostle Paul said, 'For this I labour [unto weariness], striving with all the superhuman energy which He so mightily enkindles and works within me' (Colossians 1:29 AMPB).

Doing the works of Jesus starts at home, as you unselfishly are freely willing to serve those around you.

When you daily live His life you will see His power enable you to do His works where ever you go.

Let's pray: Heavenly Father, here I am to do Your works. I trust You to enable and empower me so that all I do may give glory to Your name.

In Jesus' Name, Amen.

Don't be selfish; don't live to make a good impression on others.
Be humble, thinking of others as better than yourself
Philippians 2:3(LB)

When you are still growing in knowing the Life Jesus has with the Father, you can easily think too little of yourself and limit God. However, to think beyond your sphere of grace to impress others can be just as limiting to God. The simplicity of humility is to daily lay down your life to love and serve others.

If you humbly desire to serve God you will see opportunities all around you.

When the Lord Jesus began to reveal His work to my father, Johan Maasbach, he was in New York City, and while walking past a drunkard who was sleeping in the gutter cuddling an empty bottle, the Holy Spirit came upon my father and Jesus said to him, 'Johan, do you know you are no better than him!' At that moment Jesus filled my father's heart with His love for all the precious souls for whom He died.

While helping my father, I was always greatly impressed by his tireless love for others and remember when he said to me, 'Never forget to humble yourself, for it is within every man's heart to exalt self.'

Every opportunity to lay down your life to sweetly serve someone is an opportunity to humble yourself! Consider the humility of Jesus, who so lovingly obeyed the Father when He laid down His Life for us. Through His humility the Holy Spirit enabled Him to open the way, or better said, become the Way into the Life He has with the Father.

If you will look for opportunities to sweetly lay down your life for another you will see the Holy Spirit open the Way into the Life Jesus has with the Father through you.

Make the Heavenly Father truly happy by loving others, by serving them and being genuinely interested in their welfare for this is the Spirit of Jesus in you.

Dear child of God, the Holy Spirit will fill your heart with the love of Jesus to empower you to lay down your life to serve those around you.

Let's pray: Heavenly Father, fill me with the love of Jesus for others, empower me to lay down my life to sweetly serve them, I pray.

In Jesus' Name, Amen.

But he, wanting to justify himself, said to Jesus, 'And who is my neighbour?'

Luke 10:29

Jesus was once asked by a man, 'What shall I do to inherit eternal life?'

Jesus simply said, 'Do what God says - love the Lord your God with all your heart, soul and strength and with all your mind, and love your neighbour as yourself. If you do this you will live!'

The man feeling the pain of his failure to love others asked, 'Who is my neighbour?'

Jesus then told him a story about a Good Samaritan to ignite His compassion for others in this man (Luke 10:25-37).

Oh, how the Lord Jesus longs to ignite your heart with the fire of His love for people.

The founder of the Salvation Army, William Booth, said this:

'Will you leave them as you find them? Go, go and compassionate them (show your concern for them). Go, and present Jesus Christ to them! Go, and prophesy to them! Go, and believe for them! Go! ...and a great army shall stand up to live, fight and die for the living God. 'Not called!' did you say? 'Not heard the call,' I think you should say. Put your ear down to the Bible, and hear Him bid you go and pull sinners out of the fire of sin. Put your ear down to the burdened, agonized heart of humanity, and listen to its pitiful wail for help. Go, stand by the gates of hell, and hear the damned entreat you to go to their father's house and bid their brothers and sisters, servants and masters not to come there. Then look Christ in the face - whose mercy you have professed to obey - and tell Him whether you will join heart and soul, body and circumstances in the march to publish His mercy to the world.'

While the fire of William Booth may seem too hot to some, it is not meant to scorch you but ignite you with the love of Jesus for precious souls.

There is no greater satisfaction than to love others like Jesus and give your life to serve them in His Name.

Let's pray: Heavenly Father, fill my heart with the fire of the love of Jesus. Grant me to see a great harvest of precious souls added to Your Church. Here I am to serve You and lay down my life in love for others.

In Jesus' Name, Amen.

I indeed baptise you with water unto repentance, but He who is coming after me is mightier than I, whose sandals I am not worthy to carry. He will baptise you with the Holy Spirit and fire
Matthew 3:11

Through water baptism, we are given a great revelation of our new creation in Christ. As we are baptised in water, we are baptised into Christ. This shows that our old nature of sin has been crucified and buried with Jesus and that we have been raised with Him to live in the new creation of His heavenly Life. What a glorious gift of God in Jesus that as He lives at the throne of God so you now live through His Life in you!

The disciples saw this heavenly Life in the physical body of Jesus. They saw with their own eyes the glory of the Life Jesus has with the Father (1 John 1:1-3). So for them, water baptism was all important because they understood that it signified not only that the horrible nature of sin is buried with Jesus, but also that you have been made alive with Him to share the Life He has with the Father!

Oh, how Jesus longs for you to live in the revelation that water baptism gives.

But there is much more! Jesus not only rose from the dead to give you newness of Life in Him when you are baptised in water, He also ascended to the throne of God to baptise you with the Holy Spirit and fire.

You see when you begin to live this new Life in Him, that knows no sin or separation from the love of the Father, you will experience the baptism of the Holy Spirit and fire by which your whole nature - spirit, soul and body - is set on fire with the Life, love and power Jesus has with the Father. Here is where the ordinary person becomes extraordinary and is endowed with heavenly graces that propel them to will and do the works of God.

Jesus longs for you not merely to enjoy living the Life He gives and maintains in you, but to be on fire for the glory of God. Someone who is baptised with the Holy Spirit and fire will not stay inactive very long before this fire urges them on to greater works.

While this fire is not often visible as a flame, like on the day of Pentecost (Acts 2:3), the person highly charged with this heavenly flame does show forth a divine ability that cannot be explained as something merely earthly because it has a strong resemblance to the Life, love and power of Jesus Christ (Acts 4:13).

Let's pray: Heavenly Father, I long to live in the revelation given by water baptism of my new Life in Jesus. And oh, how I long to be baptised with the Holy Spirit and fire to propel me into greater works for Your glory.

In Jesus' Name, Amen.

Then there appeared to them divided tongues, as of fire, and one sat upon each of them

Acts 2:3

There are many things in the Old Testament that symbolise the blessings we receive in Jesus. Those who humbly sought God's face under the old covenant, were given a foretaste of things to come as they caught a glimpse of the heavenly Life.

The symbolism of the old is beautiful and inspiring, but it is not meant to obstruct our view of the true substance of things hoped for and the evidence you receive through Jesus of the riches of the glory of the heavenly Life. You see, the fire of God's holiness was always meant to light up the way into His presence where the riches of His blessings are found. In the old covenant this was indicated by the heavenly flame burning on the branches of the *menorah,* symbolising the sevenfold flame of God's Spirit, which lit up the way into the Holy of Holies. But what no eye had seen or ear had heard or the heart of man had perceived, is that God had predestined this heavenly flame to burn continually within the heart of His Church to light up the Way into His presence.

Jesus therefore taught His disciples to pray and wait before His throne of grace for the appearing of this heavenly flame. While they had seen this fire in Jesus it was marvellous and glorious to think it was now also going to burn in them forever.

Dear child of God, did you know that the Lord Jesus longs to ignite this flame in you? Before He died and rose again Jesus said, 'I came to send fire on the earth, and how I wish it were already kindled!' (Luke 12:49).

Jesus beckons you to come to His throne of grace, pray daily, and abide in His presence until your whole nature is set on fire with this glorious flame that will propel you with His love and power to do the works of God.

Remember on the day of Pentecost how a hundred and twenty men and woman who loved Jesus were praying and were set on fire with this heavenly flame.

The world has never been the same!

Today, Jesus longs to empower you with the same flame to enable you to reach the unreached and tell the untold the wonders of His great love.

Let's pray: Heavenly Father, here I am before Your throne of grace, asking now to be filled and flooded with Your Holy Spirit and set on fire for Your glory.

In Jesus' Name, Amen.

I indeed baptise you with water unto repentance, but He who is coming after me is mightier than I, whose sandals I am not worthy to carry. He will baptise you with the Holy Spirit and fire
Matthew 3:11

In the wilderness by the Jordan stood John the Baptist, clothed in camel's hair with a leather belt, crying, 'Repent, for the kingdom of heaven is at hand. He who sent me to baptise with water said to me, 'Upon whom you see the Spirit descending and remaining, this is He who will baptise you with the Holy Spirit."

The next day John saw Jesus coming toward him, and said, 'Behold the Lamb of God, who takes away the sin of the world!'

'I have seen and testified that this is the Son of God!'

'He must increase, but I must decrease. He who comes from above is above all. For whom God has sent speaks the words of God, for God does not give the Spirit by measure.'

'He will baptise you with the Holy Spirit and fire for the Father loves the Son, and has given all things into His hand. He who believes in the Son has everlasting life; and he who does not believe the Son shall not see life, but the wrath of God abides on him' (John 1:29-34, 3:31-36; Matthew 3).

Can you see the fire of God in John the Baptist as he spoke, inspired by the Holy Spirit, bearing witness that Jesus is the Christ, the Son of the living God? His witness prepared the hearts of multitudes to receive Jesus and believe in Him.

Jesus so loved John the Baptist that He said, 'I say to you, among those born of woman there has not risen one greater than John the Baptist; he bore witness of the truth, he was a burning and shining lamp, and you were willing for a time to rejoice in His light. But he who is least in the kingdom of heaven is greater than he' (Matthew 11; John 5:33, 35).

While John the Baptist is a great inspiration of what one man on fire can accomplish for God, Jesus lifts your heart to believe that the least of those who live the Life He has with the Father will burn brighter than John the Baptist.

Let's pray: Heavenly Father, how my heart yearns to be on fire with Your Spirit so I may be a witness of the Life Jesus has with You in heaven.

In Jesus' Name, Amen.

Then there appeared to them divided tongues, as of fire, and one sat upon each of them

Acts 2:3

Heaven was filled with joy when the Day of Pentecost had fully come, for God swung wide the gates of glory and poured out His promised blessing!

Suddenly there came a sound from heaven, as of a rushing mighty wind, which filled the whole house where the disciples were praying. They were all filled with the Holy Spirit and began to speak with other tongues, as the Spirit gave them utterance. People from many nations heard them speaking in their own native languages of the wonderful works of God. So they were all amazed and perplexed, saying to one another, 'Whatever could this mean?' (Acts 2).

God had foreshadowed this great heavenly blessing in the harvest festival of Pentecost.

When Israel began to enjoy the first fruits of their labour in the Promised Land, God commanded them to celebrate this festival round about May/June, fifty days after Passover. The people came before the Lord to worship Him, bringing the first fruits to celebrate His blessings. This is God's way of helping you realise that when you have been made alive with Jesus, who has entered beyond the veil of this earthly life into the presence of God for you, you will be able to enjoy the sweet fruit of His heavenly Life with the Father, a Life filled and flooded with the Holy Spirit and fire. Now on the day of Pentecost you see this gift is received by everyone who believes in Jesus, for it fulfils God's promise to Abraham that in his seed - Jesus - all the nations would be blessed (Genesis 22:18; Galatians 3:8-9).

The disciples, who were the first to celebrate this heavenly feast, were all given tongues of fire as a sign of its heavenly origin and could not but proclaim the wonderful works and miracles of God.

You see the Holy Spirit and fire is the distinguishing sign and wonder that you are a representative of the Life Jesus has with the Father.

Let's pray: Heavenly Father, Your glory is great and Your works are in all the earth and heavens. I will praise You with a tongue set on fire by Your heavenly flame.

In Jesus' Name, Amen.

For the promise is to you and to your children, and to all who are afar off, as many as the Lord our God will call

Acts 2:39

On that glorious Day of Pentecost men and woman of every walk of life were gathered. They were all of one heart, praying and believing to receive the gift of the Holy Spirit and fire.

Oh, how beautiful to see a single-minded soul with but one desire for this heavenly fire!

The Apostle Paul interceded with the Church of Corinth, as their passions were pulled upon by so many, when he said, 'I am jealous for you with a godly jealousy for I have betrothed you to one husband that I may present you as a chaste virgin to Christ' (2 Corinthians 11:2).

You see, this oneness of heart with Jesus in prayer that secured such a glorious heavenly response for those at Pentecost, is what the Saviour longs for in you to receive and maintain this heavenly flame.

Dear child of God, the Lord Jesus is calling you with these words, 'The promise is for you and your children.'

Let His love compel you to remove every distracting passion, spend time in His presence, praying like the disciples of old with one desire, to be baptised with the Holy Spirit and fire.

This single-minded prayer with Jesus is sure to secure the same results today.

Everything changed when the Holy Spirit came; the hundred and twenty precious souls in that upper room multiplied to over three thousand new converts that day.

The Holy Spirit is here. He has never left!

Jesus is seeking for hungry hearts and thirsty souls to baptise with the Holy Spirit and fire.

Let's pray: Heavenly Father, here I am in Your presence lifting holy hands to You. Perfect my loving devotion for Jesus and fill me afresh with the Holy Spirit and fire.

In Jesus' Name, Amen.

For the promise is to you and to your children, and to all who are afar off, as many as the Lord our God will call

Acts 2:39

God does everything in answer to His promise. All the promises of God in Jesus are 'Yes,' and, 'Amen, to the glory of God' (2 Corinthians 1:20).

Now your participation is vital because the ever-living Word of God is looking for your heart to be hungry so that faith can live and grow there. As it is written, 'The just shall live by faith' (Habakkuk 2:4; Romans 1:17).

God desires you to give Him your heart! That is why it is written, 'You shall love the Lord your God with all your heart, with all your soul, and with all your strength' (Deuteronomy 6:5). When you feel compelled to cry to God with all your heart and soul it is because the Lord Jesus is drawing you up into the Life He has with the Father.

When Solomon dedicated the temple to the Lord he prayed, 'Blessed be the Lord, who has given rest to His people Israel, according to all that He promised. There has not failed one word of all His good promise, which He promised through His servant Moses. May the Lord our God be with us, as He was with our fathers, may He not leave us nor forsake us, that He may incline our hearts to Himself, to walk in all His ways' (1 Kings 8:56-58).

The heart can become cold to the heavenly Life and blessings when it is over-burdened with the cares of this life, so that it has little or no real affection for Jesus. But Jesus, who is faithful as the great Apostle and High Priest of your confession, will draw you up into the Life He has with the Father so that your heart will long for the baptism of the Holy Spirit and fire.

Like a lover who stirs the heart of His beloved, Jesus compels you to seek Him while He may be found and call upon Him while He is near.

Be greatly encouraged, dear child of God, as you set yourself to seek the Lord, for He will be very merciful to you, abundantly pardon you and show you the light of His countenance in the baptism of the Holy Spirit and fire.

Let's pray: Heavenly Father, I set myself to seek Your face; incline my heart toward You so that I may always walk in Your ways, in the baptism of the Holy Spirit and fire.

In Jesus' Name, Amen.

Therefore He who supplies the Spirit to you and works miracles among you, does He do it by the works of the law, or by the hearing of faith?

Galatians 3:4

What heavenly joy, that when you hear the good news about Jesus and believe in Him you receive the Holy Spirit!

You see the Holy Spirit comes in answer to the Life Jesus has with the Father.

Jesus said about the Holy Spirit, 'He will glorify Me, for He will take of what is Mine and declare it to you. All things that the Father has are Mine. Therefore I said that He will take of Mine and declare it to you' (John 16:14, 15).

The Holy Spirit does not come in answer to any good deed you have done but in answer to the Life Jesus has with the Father. This is why when you hear about Jesus and believe in Him, you receive this wonderful gift.

You can clearly see this when Peter was preaching at Cornelius' house in Caesarea. While he was still telling them about Jesus, all who heard the words Peter spoke about Jesus and believed in Him were baptised with the Holy Spirit and fire. The fire may not have been visible on the outside, like on the Day of Pentecost, but it was obviously living on the inside, since all who received the Holy Spirit began to speak with tongues and magnified God. Peter had no doubt that they had all received the same Holy Spirit just as he had (Acts 10:47).

Jesus told His disciples that they would receive power when the Holy Spirit came upon them to enable them to tell everyone about Him.

You see, the Holy Spirit comes to reveal the Life and blessings Jesus has with the Father.

He helps you to speak about Jesus and to convince those who hear you to believe in Him and be saved.

Let's pray: Heavenly Father, help me in the power of the Holy Spirit to tell others about Jesus. Convince those who hear me, I pray, to believe in Him and be saved.

In Jesus' Name, Amen.

Who, when they had come down, prayed for them that they might receive the Holy Spirit

Acts 8:15

What God is able to do for those who pray is beyond measure!

When Jesus prayed, heaven opened and the Holy Spirit came upon Him (Luke 3:21-22).

Jesus took off all the limits when He prayed. Not only were the heavens opened but He was also transfigured. Moses and Elijah were seen talking with Him and the Father overshadowed them to reveal the glory Jesus has with Him in heaven (Luke 9:27-35).

Dear child of God, let the Life of Jesus daily draw you up in prayer to the throne of God so that you may be filled with the Holy Spirit.

You see a prayer-less life is a merely earthly life; it shows you are unaware of the blessings of Life that are available to you in heaven.

King David longed for a Spirit-filled life when he prayed, 'O God, You are my God, earnestly will I seek You; my inner self thirsts for You, my flesh longs and is faint for You, in a dry and weary land where there is no water. So I have looked upon You in the sanctuary to see Your power and Your glory. Because Your loving-kindness is better than life, my lips shall praise You. So will I bless You while I live; I will lift up my hands in Your name. My whole being shall be satisfied as with marrow and fatness; and my mouth shall praise You with joyful lips' (Psalm 63:1-5 AMPB).

God desires your whole being to be satisfied with the Holy Spirit!

The marrow and fatness is the Holy Spirit's anointing in your bones and flesh.

While such a Spirit-filled life may feel as far away from you as it did for King David, if, like him, you begin to pray, before long you will see the heavens opened and the Holy Spirit come upon you.

Pray, pray, pray and give God all the praise.

Sing to Him a new song and be filled with the Holy Spirit.

Let's pray: Heavenly Father, I know it is Your good pleasure to give me the Holy Spirit. Here I am in Your presence lifting holy hands to You.

In Jesus' Name, Amen.

For as yet He had fallen upon none of them. They had only been baptised in the name of the Lord Jesus

Acts 8:16

In the days after Pentecost, people who believed in Jesus received the Holy Spirit but not all in the same way. Many had been believers in Jesus for some time and had enjoyed His miracles by the hearing of faith and the laying on of hands by those who ministered in Jesus' name. While this was the work of the Holy Spirit, they had not yet been baptised with the Holy Spirit (Acts 8:6, 16).

Dear child of God, there is so much Jesus desires to share with you from the Life He has with the Father. There are not enough days on earth to receive it all. Praise God we have all eternity to sing His praises for the glory He has called us to share in Him (Ephesians 2:7).

One of the most important gifts Jesus gives is the Holy Spirit who proceeds from the Father.

Remember, all Jesus gives comes forth from the Father (John 15:26).

One hundred and twenty men and woman in the upper room on the Day of Pentecost received the Holy Spirit while in prayer. Others heard the gospel about Jesus, repented, were baptised in water and then received the Holy Spirit. Again others while hearing the gospel about Jesus were filled with the Holy Spirit and then were baptised in water. Others received this gift while they were prayed for and while hands were laid on them.

No one should limit God in how He is to give His gifts, for all may receive freely, without reproach.

We must never forget that God saved us not because of the good things we did but because of His great mercy. He washed away our sins and gave us a new life through the Holy Spirit. He generously poured out the Spirit upon us because of what Jesus Christ our Saviour did (Titus 3:5-7 NLT).

Let's pray: Heavenly Father, I know You love me, thank you for giving me faith in Jesus and the gift of the Holy Spirit.
In Jesus' Name, Amen.

The Holy Spirit, whom He poured out on us abundantly through Jesus Christ our Saviour

Titus 3:5-6

Look to Jesus and be filled with the Holy Spirit! For out of the fullness of the Life He has with the Father the Holy Spirit is poured out on you abundantly.

Consider the Prophet Elijah, how through his prayers the heavens gave forth rain on a dry and thirsty land (James 5:18). Even so, Jesus at the throne of God ever lives to make intercession to give you the Holy Spirit. This is why Jesus said, 'But when the Helper comes, whom I shall send to you from the Father, the Spirit of truth who proceeds from the Father, He will testify of me' (John 15:26).

The Spirit-filled Life is wonderful, powerful and so full of glory! The extent of this glory is beyond our comprehension. We cannot yet fully see what we will be like when we see the Father and are made perfect in His likeness, but we do see Jesus who is our Life with the Father (Colossians 3:4). When you receive the Holy Spirit you begin to taste and see the glory of the Life Jesus has with the Father (Hebrews 6:4-5).

Jesus said, 'When the Holy Spirit has come upon you, you will be witnesses of me' (Acts 1:8).

Can you think of any greater privilege than to be a witness of the Life Jesus has with the Father?

You see the Holy Spirit comes with immeasurable grace and gifts, all of which bear witness of the fullness of the Life Jesus has with the Father.

Be encouraged, dear child of God, for it is the Father's great pleasure to give you the Holy Spirit and enable you to come to the fullness of the stature of Jesus (Ephesians 4:13).

To be a witness of Jesus is the greatest glory any human being can have on earth.

As it is written, 'Thus says the LORD: 'Let not the wise man glory in his wisdom. Let not the mighty man glory in his might. Nor let the rich man glory in his riches. But let him who glories glory in this, that he understands and knows Me" (Jeremiah 9:23-24).

Let's pray: Heavenly Father, I worship You! I thank You for filling me with the Holy Spirit and granting me the privilege to glory in knowing You in all I am, say and do.

In Jesus' Name, Amen.

When the Helper comes, whom I shall send to you from the Father, the Spirit of truth who proceeds from the Father, He will testify of me

John 15:26

For your natural mind to understand the greatness of the glory of the Life Jesus lives in the Holy Spirit who proceeds from the Father, is like asking a bird to comprehend the heavens in which it flies, or a fish the vastness of the oceans in which it swims.

When the great prophet Isaiah saw the glory of the Life Jesus has with the Father, he cried, 'Oh Lord, even if I do Your miracles, who would believe me if I tell them of this Life?' (John 12:37-41).

But you see, this is exactly why Jesus became a man, suffered, died, rose again and ascended to the throne of God, so that through the Life He has with the Father, He can open your understanding to the Holy Spirit who proceeds from the Father, and forever end the struggle of sin that darkened your heart with death by the absence of this Life.

Be encouraged, dear child of God, for Jesus said that the Holy Spirit will help you. 'He will testify to the Life I have with the Father. He will heal your heart and enable you to believe and enter by faith into the full flow of this Life. For the Holy Spirit who proceeds from the Father will become like a river flowing from your heart. He will enable you to realise through experience this Life that knows no sin or falling short of the Father's glory, nor separation from His great love.'

Jesus said, 'When the Holy Spirit has come in you, then you will know that I am in the Father and you in Me and I in you' (John 14:16-20).

The Heavenly Father desires for you to live in the full flow of the Holy Spirit who proceeds from Him, so that He can enable you to live on earth as Jesus lives at the throne.

Let's pray: Heavenly Father, here I am to live in the full flow of the Holy Spirit who proceeds from You.

In Jesus' Name, Amen.

When the Helper comes whom I shall send to you from the Father, the Spirit of truth who proceeds from the Father, He will testify of Me

John 15:26

Dear child of God, let your tender heart of faith find perfect rest in Jesus, for the Holy Spirit who proceeds forth from the Father comes to you through the Life He has with the Father.

Consider Jesus, who for the love of the Father, while you were yet a sinner, was freely willing to take away all your sins in His own blood when He died. Now if Jesus did so much for you while you were yet a sinner by dying for you, how much more now that you are His child will He do for you through the Life He has with the Father!

Be encouraged, for every good gift, every blessing, yes the Holy Spirit Himself who proceeds from the Father, is yours through your union with Jesus (Ephesians 1:3; Colossians 2:9-10).

Just as the sun never ceases to shine forth its light and warmth, so Christ at the throne of God never stops giving forth the Life He has with the Father by giving you the Holy Spirit (Acts 2:33).

Most rivers are formed by rain and snow on high mountains. While it might be dead and dry in the valley, the river is in full flow because of where it comes from.

Even so, the Holy Spirit coming forth from the Father is in full flow in you because of Jesus.

As it is written, 'He opened the rock (Christ), and water gushed out; It ran in the dry places like a river' (Psalm 105:41).

Jesus said if you are thirsty (if you feel merely earthly), come and drink (John 7:37-38).

You see, this is why Jesus is at the throne of God, so He can continually fill and flood you with the Holy Spirit.

You can trust Jesus; He will not fail you, for the Holy Spirit who proceeds forth from the Father will flow through you like a river because of the Life Jesus has with the Father.

Let's pray: Heavenly Father, I worship You for the Life and love of Jesus that make it possible for the Holy Spirit to flow like a river through my heart.

In Jesus' Name, Amen.

He will glorify Me, for He will take of what is Mine and declare it to you

John 16:14

Jesus showed that the Holy Spirit will take the Life He has with the Father and reveal it to you. He said, 'All things that the Father has are Mine. Therefore I said that He (the Holy Spirit) will take of Mine and declare it to you' (John 16:15).

The way Jesus talked about the Holy Spirit was a heavenly language which comes from a mindset that knows no sin, for only the sin nature makes you think separate from God.

Jesus spoke the words the Father taught Him when He said, 'All things that the Father has are Mine' (John 16:15).

Dear child of God, the Father desires you to be of one heart and mind with Him and to know that the Life Jesus has with Him at the throne is what He now gives to you.

This is why Jesus said, 'When the Holy Spirit has come you will know that I am in My Father, and you in Me, and I in you' (John 14:20).

You see, the Holy Spirit will help you become one with the Father and the Son.

Consider the greatness of your salvation when Jesus said, 'I in them and You in Me, all being perfected into one - so that the world will know You sent Me and will understand that You love them as much as You love Me' (John 17:23 LB).

When you read these words of Jesus you may realise why the apostles who represented Him would say, 'I count everything as loss compared to the possession of the priceless privilege (the overwhelming preciousness, the surpassing worth, and supreme advantage) of knowing Christ Jesus my Lord. And that I may [actually] be found and known as in Him, [For my determined purpose is] that I may know Him [that I may progressively become more deeply and intimately acquainted with Him, perceiving and recognising and understanding the wonders of His Person more strongly and more clearly], as to be continually transformed [in spirit into His likeness]' (Philippians 3:8-10 AMPB).

Let's pray: Heavenly Father, it overwhelms me to know You love me as You love Jesus, and that You grant me to share the Life He has with You through the Holy Spirit. I love You, Father, for loving me so much.

In Jesus' Name, Amen.

When the Helper comes, whom I shall send to you from the Father, the Spirit of truth who proceeds from the Father, He will testify of Me

John 15:26

Jesus called the Holy Spirit the 'Spirit of truth' because He proceeds from the Father to reveal Him. Jesus Himself is Truth for it pleased the Father that in Him the fullness of Himself would dwell (Colossians 2:15, 19). Now this Life Jesus has in the Father is what the Holy Spirit gives so that you may know God inwardly (John 14:20)!

King David prayed, 'Behold, You desire truth in my inner being' (Psalm 51:6). 'O God, You are my God, earnestly will I seek You; my inner self thirsts for You, my flesh longs and is faint for You, in a dry and weary land where there is no water' (Psalm 63:1 AMPB).

You see, to know God with your understanding is to limit Him, for no one knows the things of God except the Spirit of God (1 Corinthians 2:11).

Consider therefore the greatness of the Father's love for you, that He gives the Holy Spirit so you may know Him inwardly and can worship Him in spirit and truth.

Whenever Jesus talked about knowing the Father He spoke from what was in Him as the Holy Spirit in Him bore witness to the Life He has with the Father.

Now this is what Jesus meant when He said, 'the truth will set you free' (John 8:32). This is true freedom from sin, that you are no longer self-conscious, thinking as if you were separated from the Father and still falling short of His glory. No, you are now free from sin because you know the Father inwardly by the Spirit of truth and you have the mind of Christ.

This is the intercession of Jesus at the throne of God, that you may really come to 'know practically, through experience for yourselves, the love of Christ which far surpasses mere knowledge [without experience]; that you may be filled [through all your being] unto all the fullness of God [may have the richest measure of the divine Presence, and become a body wholly filled and flooded with God Himself]! (Ephesians 3:19 AMPB).

Let's pray: Heavenly Father, how great You are! Then sings my soul, my Saviour God to You; how great You are for revealing Yourself in me by the Holy Spirit, the Spirit of truth who proceeds from You.

In Jesus' Name, Amen.

When the Helper comes, whom I shall send to you from the Father, the Spirit of truth who proceeds from the Father, He will testify of Me

John 15:26

Jesus is God revealed. The words He spoke bring God's Life- giving Spirit (John 1:18; 6:63).

Jesus said, 'For this cause I was born, and for this cause I have come into the world, that I should bear witness to the truth. Everyone who is of the truth hears My voice' (John 18:37).

You see you know you have the Spirit of truth in you when the Life you live bears witness to Jesus. The beloved Apostle John, like the other apostles, always contended for the truth that all who have the Son have eternal Life (1 John 5:12).

John said, 'You will know the truth when the Spirit who is in you teaches you to abide in Jesus, for he who acknowledges the Son has the Father also' (1 John 2:27, 23).

Dear child of God, you do not ever need to struggle with your identity.

Consider Jesus, who was questioned and even tempted about who He was but never wondered about His identity. He knew inwardly He was the Son of God for He knew that the Life He lived in the body came from the Father (John 7:57).

Jesus believed the Spirit of truth who testified to His Life in the Father and the Father in Him.

Even so, the Holy Spirit reveals the truth of the Life Jesus has with the Father in you so you may know who you are as His child (Romans 8:16).

Whether you are born in a palace or a manger the big question is - are you born of God?

When the Apostle Paul met Jesus, he was born again; he became a brand new person on the inside; the Life Jesus has with the Father came into him, and from then on he knew God inwardly.

The moment the Spirit of truth bore witness to Christ in him Paul's perspective of himself changed completely. Once he thought he was superior to others (Philippians 3:4-6) but as a new creation, born of God, Paul said, 'I have been crucified with Christ; it is no longer I who live, but Christ lives in me; and the life which I now live in the flesh I live by faith in the Son of God, who loved me and gave Himself for me' (Galatians 2:20).

Let's pray: Heavenly Father, Your Spirit bears witness in me to the truth that the Life Jesus has with You is in me. I know I am Your child for I know that the Life that is in me comes from You!

In Jesus' Name, Amen.

He will glorify Me, for He will take of what is Mine and declare it to you

John 16:14

The Holy Spirit is also called the Spirit of glory (1 Peter 4:14). Jesus said, 'The Holy Spirit will glorify Me for He will take the Life I have with the Father and reveal it in you.'

You see it is God's promise that because you are His child you have become an heir together with Jesus of everything He has with the Father (Romans 8:16-17).

Since the Life you now live comes from the throne of God, set your affections on Jesus and make no provision for the flesh to fulfil its lusts (Romans 13:14) but let your roots of faith and expectation grow deep into Jesus Christ Himself as you draw your nourishment, satisfaction and fulfilment from your union with Him (Colossians 2:6-7).

Before you knew Jesus you were led astray in the pursuit of things that do not give life, but now that you have the Holy Spirit you know your Life comes from Jesus (John 6:57). Now your whole life shines forth with His Life.

King David filled with the Holy Spirit cried out, 'How long, O you sons of men, will you turn My glory to shame? How long will you love worthlessness and seek falsehood? (Why worship what gives no life) Selah [pause, and calmly think of that]! But know that the Lord has set apart for Himself him who is godly (The man of loving-kindness); the Lord will hear when I call to Him' (Psalm 4:2-3 AMPB).

The Holy Spirit, the Spirit of glory, yearns in you with jealousy, with indescribable feelings for the riches of the glory of the Life Jesus has with the Father to be revealed in you (Romans 8:26).

The more you learn to yield to the Holy Spirit's yearning, the more you will grow in the knowledge of Jesus the Son of God and will see the glory of His Life formed in you, until you are filled with the measure of the stature of the fullness of Christ and become a body wholly filled and flooded with God Himself (Ephesians 4:13, 3:19).

Let's pray: Heavenly Father, may I never turn Your glory to shame by loving worthlessness and seeking falsehood. For You, O Lord, are a shield for me.

In Jesus' Name, Amen.

He will glorify Me, for He will take of what is Mine and declare it to you

John 16:14

The coming of the Holy Spirit is the great fulfilment of God's promise (Genesis 22:18; Acts 2:33) for He reveals the glory of the Life Jesus has with the Father to which you are called (Romans 8:29-30; John 17:22-23).

There is no real glory for anyone outside of Jesus (1 Corinthians 1:30-31).

Anything less than His Life in you will always make you feel you are lacking and falling short of God's glory (Romans 3:23).

Jesus said, 'He, the Holy Spirit, will glorify Me, for He will take of what is Mine and declare it to you!' So you see it is only the Holy Spirit who can give you to share the glory of the Life Jesus has with the Father.

Dear child of God, Jesus is the promise of the Father fulfilled. He is the Seed of Abraham through whom God promised to bless the whole world (Galatians 3:8-16).

The Holy Spirit who proceeds from the Father can only come to you so generously and continuously because of Jesus. And only the Holy Spirit can perfect your heart's affections and renew your mind to have the mind of Christ, so you can become an unobstructed channel for an unhindered flow of His Life in glory.

Be encouraged, for the Father longs for you to live filled with the Holy Spirit, so He may clothe you with garments white as snow, which is no less than the glory of the Life Jesus has with the Father. God will do all this for you so that your life on earth is to the praise of His glory for all He has done for you through Jesus (Matthew 5:16; Ephesians 2:6-7).

Believe that you are called by God to show forth His glory through the Life of Jesus in you, for Jesus alone is the ever-living hope of eternal Life for the whole world.

'Now may the God of peace Himself sanctify you completely; and may your whole spirit, soul, and body be preserved blameless at the coming of our Lord Jesus Christ. He who calls you is faithful, who also will do it' (1 Thessalonians 5:23-24).

Let's pray: Heavenly Father, I know You are faithful to sanctify my whole spirit, soul and body through the Life of Jesus in me so I may show forth Your glory.

In Jesus' Name, Amen.

So, when he had gone out, Jesus said, 'Now the Son of Man is glorified, and God is glorified in Him'

John 13:31

Jesus often called Himself the 'Son of Man' because He who came from heaven was glad to be revealed as a human being (John 1:14; Colossians 1:19).

God said, 'Let us make man in our image, according to our likeness. So God created man; male and female He created them' (Genesis 1:26-27).

You see, even as Jesus became the Son of Man and we saw in Him the glory of the Life He has with the Father, so God has called you to share His glory by the Holy Spirit living and abiding in you - making His permanent home in your heart - so that you may have the inner strength of the Holy Spirit, through faith, to know and recognise His Life in you and others (Ephesians 3:14-19).

Did you know that every time you pray, 'Our Father in heaven, hallowed be Your name,' you are asking Him to be glorified in you (Matthew 6:9)?

Dear child of God, the Father longs to see you glorified with the Life Jesus has with Him. This is why He gives you the Holy Spirit (John 7:39).

Remember Jesus said, 'The Holy Spirit will glorify Me, for He will take of what is Mine and declare it to you' (John 16:14).

If it was not for the Life Jesus has with the Father, then all we would have of the image of God would be types and shadows, but in Jesus the fullness of His glory is not only revealed but imparted.

This is why Jesus prayed, 'I have given them the glory You gave Me - the glorious unity of being one, as we are - I in them and You in Me, all being perfected into one - so that the world will know You sent Me and will understand that You love them as much as You love Me. Father, I want them with Me - these You've given Me - so that they can see My glory. You gave Me the glory because You loved Me before the world began. O righteous Father, the world doesn't know You, but I do; and these disciples know You sent Me. And I have revealed You to them and will keep on revealing You so that the mighty love You have for Me may be in them, and I in them' (John 17:22-26 LB).

Now even as you have borne the image of the man of dust, so you will bear the image of the heavenly man (1 Corinthians 15:49).

Let's pray: Heavenly Father, strengthen me inwardly with Your mighty power through the Holy Spirit living in me, so I may know and recognise through faith, the glory of the Life of Jesus Christ in me and others.

In Jesus' Name, Amen.

But the Helper, the Holy Spirit, whom the Father will send in My name, He will teach you all things, and bring to your remembrance all things that I said to you

John 14:26-27

Jesus said, 'There is so much I want to tell you about my Life in the Father but you cannot bear it now but when the Holy Spirit comes He will teach you all things' (John 16:12-13).

Often Jesus spoke in parables and figures of speech to give earthly comparisons to His heavenly Life. Like when He said to Nicodemus, you must be born again, or when He gave the parable about abiding in the vine, or eating His flesh and drinking His blood. These thoughts make perfect sense for someone filled with the Holy Spirit but they are difficult to comprehend for those who do not have the Spirit. You see there is only so much your natural mind can take in without the Holy Spirit, but through the indwelling presence of the Holy Spirit you are given the mind of Christ so that you may know what is freely given you in the Life He has with the Father (1 Corinthians 2:12-16).

Oh dear child of God, let the Holy Spirit teach you, for He who proceeds from the Father will guide you into all the truth of the Life Jesus has in the Father and impart it to you.

There is no need for you to live in darkness and wonder about the riches of the glory of His Life. The Holy Spirit has come and He will help you! You may say, 'Yes, but how will He help me? How will He teach me and give me the mind of Christ?'

Trust in Jesus; ask the Father and He will give you the Holy Spirit!

You know the Holy Spirit has come to you because your spirit is made alive with Jesus; the Scriptures open up to you; God speaks directly to you through His Word. And when you pray, the Holy Spirit helps you to enjoy intimate fellowship with the Father.

There are so many wonderful graces, gifts and blessings that begin to fill your life when the Holy Spirit comes that you will never see the end of it. Yes, the blessings of the Holy Spirit who proceeds from the Father are endless and glorious.

Let's pray: Heavenly Father, fill me with the Holy Spirit and teach me to have the mind of Christ Jesus so I may know what You have freely given me through His Life in me.

In Jesus' Name, Amen.

But the anointing which you have received from Him abides in you, and you do not need that anyone teach you; but as the same anointing teaches you concerning all things, and is true, and is not a lie, and just as it has taught you, you will abide in Him.

1 John 2:26-27

The Holy Spirit living in you is what we call 'the anointing.' His blessed presence gives you the identity of the Father from whom the Holy Spirit comes.

When the Apostles Peter and John were filled with the Holy Spirit, people marvelled at the boldness by which they spoke about Jesus. Though they were fisherman from Galilee, everyone could see they had been with Jesus because the image that emanated from them was the same Life of the Father that shone from Jesus (Acts 4:13).

This, dear child of God, no one can teach you but the Holy Spirit.

Only the Holy Spirit who proceeds from the Father is able to teach you to abide in the Life Jesus has with Him (John 14:19-23).

Jesus said, 'As it is written in the Scriptures, 'They shall all be taught of God.' Those the Father speaks to, who learn the truth from Him, will be attracted to Me. (Not that anyone actually sees the Father, for only I have seen Him.) How earnestly I tell you this - anyone who believes in Me already has eternal life!' (John 6:44-47 LB).

The Holy Spirit, who proceeds from the Father, forms the Life Jesus has with Him in you and this becomes evident by virtue of the fact that you know God inwardly, you have heard His voice and His Word lives in you.

The Life Jesus has with the Father is the light of all man. Without His light of Life you live in darkness and don't know God (John 1:4, 9).

Praise, glory and honour to Jesus Christ our God and Saviour, for you do know God, for He lives in you. The same Life you see in Jesus is now also in you.

So you see, you are anointed! You have the indwelling blessed presence of the Holy Spirit, who is continuously teaching you to know, perceive and recognise the truth inwardly.

Let me say this again, you are anointed! You do know God for the same Life that emanated from Jesus is in you.

Let's pray: Heavenly Father, what grace, what riches of glory, that You would anoint me with the blessed presence of the Holy Spirit so that in all I am, say and do I may know You.

In Jesus' Name, Amen.

The Spirit of the Lord shall rest upon Him, the Spirit of wisdom and understanding, the Spirit of counsel and might, the Spirit of knowledge and of the fear of the Lord

Isaiah 11:2

The Holy Spirit is foreshadowed as a sevenfold flame (Exodus 25:31-40).

John the beloved saw this seven fold flame at the throne of God in Jesus (Revelation 1:4, 4:5, 5:6).

So when you think about the anointing, look to Jesus who clearly characterised this heavenly flame in the grace and truth by which the Holy Spirit gave Him such heavenly wisdom and understanding, counsel and might, knowledge and the fear of the Lord, and the oil of gladness (Psalm 45:7). Jesus never judged anyone by what He saw or heard for His delight was in the fear of the Lord (John 8:15-16; Isaiah 11:3).

The Holy Spirit gave Jesus wisdom and stature so that only God's goodness poured forth and many hearing Him were astonished, saying, 'Where did this man get these things? And what wisdom is this which is given to Him, that such mighty works are performed by His hands?' (Mark 6:2).

When Jesus talked about the anointing He said, 'The Spirit of the Lord is upon Me because He has anointed Me.' Then He said, 'Today this Scripture is fulfilled in Your hearing' (Luke 4:18, 21). The understanding the Holy Spirit gave Jesus enabled Him to open the scriptures and show the mind of God (Luke 24:27, 31-32). It is beautiful to see the anointing in Jesus, for by the counsel of the Holy Spirit He always knew what to do, and by the might of the Spirit He was able to do it.

You can clearly see the oil of gladness in Him as His delight was in the fear of the Lord. In other words Jesus' satisfaction was in doing the will of the Father (John 4:34; Hebrews 5:7).

The anointing you see in Jesus takes off all the limits for the Father to reveal Himself.

Oh, how the Father longs to anoint you with the Holy Spirit so you may be able to do the works Jesus does and see the Father glorified through His Son in you (John 14:12-13).

Let's pray: Heavenly Father, I long to live anointed with the Holy Spirit so I may not judge anyone by what I see or hear. I long to continue on earth what You started in Jesus so all nations may see Your glory.

In Jesus' Name, Amen.

How God anointed Jesus of Nazareth with the Holy Spirit and with power, who went about doing good and healing all who were oppressed by the devil, for God was with Him

Acts 10:38-39

Jesus said, 'You shall receive power when the Holy Spirit has come upon you' (Acts 1:8).

You can clearly see this power in Peter when, filled with the Holy Spirit, he began to speak about Jesus to a mocking hostile crowd and three thousand of them were struck to the heart with conviction, repented of their sins, received Jesus, were baptised in water and filled with the Holy Spirit (Acts 2).

The Holy Spirit anoints ordinary people with power to do extraordinary things.

History goes on to tell of those anointed with power who like Jesus went about doing good, healing all who were oppressed by the devil.

Today Jesus is calling you!

But you may say, 'How can I have this anointing of power?'

One of the characteristics of those who have received this anointing of power is prayer.

A place called Filey (UK) was given up to ungodliness in the early days of Methodism. Preacher after preacher was sent there but to no avail, until the now famous John Oxtoby, better known as 'Praying Johnny', pleaded to give Filey one more chance. Johnny was sent there. While he was on his way someone who knew him asked, 'Where are you going?' Johnny replied, 'To Filey, where the Lord is going to revive His work.' When Filey came into view the feelings of despair were so overwhelming that Johnny fell to his knees and cried out in prayer, 'You can't make a fool of me. I have told everyone You are going to revive Your work. If You don't then I will never be able to show my face again for what will people think about praying and believing?' Johnny wrestled in agonizing prayer for several hours. The struggle was long and heavy but he would not cease to pray as his sense of powerlessness was his plea. At length, the dark clouds dispersed, the glory of Jesus filled his soul as His power began to flow from his heart. Johnny arose exclaiming, 'It is done, Lord. It is done. Filey is taken!' And taken it was, and all in it, make no mistake. Fresh from the mercy-seat, Johnny entered Filey singing songs of praise. Hardened sinners hearing him were struck to the heart with conviction and cried aloud for mercy and found it. The Lord's work in Filey was revived and God was glorified.

Jesus is calling you - as a lost, sighing, dying world awaits Him to revive His work.

Let's pray: Heavenly Father, grant me a burden for souls; help me to pray and fill me today with the Holy Spirit and power to see Your work revived.

In Jesus' Name, Amen.

Now He who establishes us with you in Christ and has anointed us is God

2 Corinthians 1:21

The apostles knew the reason so many people received them was because when they began to talk about Jesus God anointed them with the Holy Spirit and power.

They would never have dared to think that this was through their own capabilities since they knew their ability was God working through them (2 Corinthians 3:4-5).

The Apostle Paul said, 'When I came to You, I was weak and trembled all over with fear, and my teaching and message were not delivered with skilful words of human wisdom, but with convincing proof of the power of God's Spirit. Your faith, then, does not rest on human wisdom but on God's power' (1 Corinthians 2:3-5 TEV).

When Peter and John were on their way to pray, a man in his forties who was born lame was healed. When all the people saw this Peter said, 'Why do you marvel at this? Or why look so intently at us, as though by our own power or godliness we had made this man walk? God glorified His Servant Jesus and His name, through faith in His name, has made this man strong, whom you see and know. Yes, the faith which comes through Him has given him this perfect soundness in the presence of you all' (Acts 3:12-16).

You see the Holy Spirit and power serve a very important purpose. They help people to 'have faith in God' (Mark 11:22). God will demonstrate His power when you talk about Jesus, so that all who hear you may receive faith in God.

Jesus, mightily anointed with the Holy Spirit and power, prayed, 'I have told these men all about You. Now they know that everything I have is a gift from You, for I have passed on to them the words You gave Me; and they accepted them and know that I came from You, and they believe You sent Me' (John 17:6-8 NLT). Jesus knew that God had anointed Him with power in order to help those who heard Him to have faith in God.

Now God has anointed you with the Holy Spirit and power so that you may speak His word and so that all those who hear you may 'have faith in God!'

Let's pray: Heavenly Father, all the good things I have come from You. You are all I have and You give me all I need; how wonderful are Your gifts to me; how good they are!

In Jesus' Name, Amen.

And I will pray the Father, and He will give you another Helper,
that He may abide with you forever

John 14:16

Your heart has all the help it needs to 'have faith in God.' For
Jesus, who is exalted to the right hand of God, has received from
the Father the promised Holy Spirit whom He now gives to abide
with you forever (Acts 2:33).

Because you live in a temporal earthen body, the faith you have to
live as He lives is given and maintained through the intercession
of His Life with the Father (Hebrews 7:25).

And the faith I am talking about is the same faith by which Jesus
lived His heavenly Life on earth. Jesus said, 'As the living Father
sent Me, and I live because of the Father, so he who feeds on Me
will live because of Me' (John 6:57).

As you come to know Jesus better, you will know His divine
power gives you everything you need for living a truly godly life
on earth. For you will know through experience for yourself His
mighty power by which He gives you all the rich and wonderful
promises in His Word (2 Peter 1:3-4).

One of those exceedingly great and most precious promises that
gives your heart the faith you see in Jesus is, 'As for Me, this is
My promise to them,' says the Lord, 'My Holy Spirit shall not
leave them, and they shall want the good and hate the wrong -
they and their children and their children's children forever'
(Isaiah 59:21 LB).

You see the moment your heart is filled with the Life of Jesus by
the indwelling presence of the Holy Spirit, all else becomes mere
loss - like chasing the wind - compared to the priceless privilege
of knowing His Life in you.

The Life of Jesus Christ in you will always compel you to live for Him, to love what is good and turn from evil.

Oh, how it pleases the Father to see you live in His righteousness, peace and joy by the power of the Holy Spirit (Romans 14:17-18).

Let's pray: Heavenly Father, thank You for helping me! Thank You for giving me the Holy Spirit! I love living by the same faith Jesus lived His heavenly Life on earth.

In Jesus' Name, Amen.

*You have loved righteousness and hated lawlessness; therefore
God, Your God, has anointed You with the oil of gladness more
than your companions*

Hebrews 1:9

God was addressing His Son Jesus as God when He said,
'O God, Your throne will last for all eternity; and You will
rule with authority in Your Kingdom because of Your
righteousness. For You have loved what is right and hated
what is evil. For this reason I, Your God, have set You above
all others by anointing You with the oil of joy.'

King David spoke by the Holy Spirit of this oil of joy when God
anointed him to reign.

He said, 'The king is glad, O Lord, because You gave him strength;
he rejoices because You made him victorious. Your blessings are
with him forever and Your presence fills him with joy. The king
trusts in the Lord Almighty; and because of the Lord's constant
love he will always be secure' (Psalm 21:1-7 TEV).

David prophesied about Jesus when he said, 'The Spirit of the
Lord spoke by me, and His word was on my tongue. The Rock
of Israel said to me, 'One shall come who rules righteously, who
rules in the fear of God. He shall be as the light of the morning"
(2 Samuel 23:2-4 LB).

The joy of Jesus reigning at the throne of God is the anointing
with which He longs for you to reign with Him on earth. As it
is written, 'All who receive God's abundant grace and are
freely put right with Him will rule in Life through Christ' (Romans
5:17 TEV).

'The Lord (God) says to my Lord (the Messiah); sit at My right hand, until I make Your adversaries Your footstool' (Psalm 110:1 AMPB).

You see, Jesus reigns far above all principalities and powers, all might and dominion, and every name that is named, not only in this age but also in that which is to come. And God put all things under His feet, and gave Him to be head over all things to the church, which is His body, the fullness of Him who fills all in all (Ephesians 1:21-23).

Now when His anointing comes on you, you will know the joy of His reign in the love and kindness of God our Saviour toward man. You will know God's mercy by which He saves through the washing of regeneration and the renewing of the Holy Spirit, whom He pours out abundantly through His reign (Titus 3:4-7).

Nothing is more powerful and wonderful on earth than to reign with Jesus in the fullness of the joy of His Life with the Father (Psalm 16:11).

Let's pray: Heavenly Father, I worship You, I bow down and yield myself to You; I want to be full of that oil of joy in which Jesus reigns at Your throne. I love You Father!

In Jesus' Name, Amen.

The One whom God has sent speaks God's words, because God gives Him the fullness of His Spirit

John 3:34 (TEV)

When you think of those whom God anointed throughout the Bible, Moses stands out as he was found faithful in God's house as a servant to illustrate the things that would happen in the future (Hebrews 3:5). Moses spoke about Jesus when God said to him, 'I will raise up for them a Prophet like you from among their brethren, and will put my words in His mouth, and He shall speak to them all that I command Him' (Deuteronomy 18:18).

You see Jesus was given the Spirit without measure because He only spoke the Life-giving words the Father taught Him (John 5:19). Today, Jesus longs for you to live a life anointed with the Holy Spirit and learn to speak Life-giving words.

At first the words of God were written on tablets of stone which is symbolic of the heart of man hardened by the sin nature. But in Jesus there is no sin; the Word is made flesh and the glory of His Life with the Father is clearly revealed in the Words He spoke (John 1:14). Jesus said, 'The words I say are not My own but are from My Father who lives in Me' (John 14:10 LB). Jesus prayed, 'Father, I have given to them the words which You have given Me; and they have received them, and have known surely that I came forth from You; and they have believed that You sent Me' (John 17:8).

It is perfectly clear - now that you are made alive with Jesus, His word lives, abides and is active in you (1 Peter 1:23) so that you have the Holy Spirit's anointing to speak, through His Life in you, Life-giving words.

When you think about being anointed with the Holy Spirit, think about speaking Life-giving words so that everyone who hears you receives Him who lives in you.

Jesus said to the Apostle Peter what He is now saying to you, 'Go, stand and speak the words of this Life' (Acts 5:20).

Let's pray: Heavenly Father, open my ears; given me an understanding heart; anoint me with Your Holy Spirit; teach me to speak Your Life-giving words so that all who hear me may receive Your Life.

In Jesus' Name, Amen.

Now concerning spiritual gifts, brethren, I do not want you to be ignorant

1 Corinthians 12:1

In Jesus you see the fullness of the Holy Spirit expressed in innumerable gifts revealing the Life He has with the Father (John 10:38). Every good gift and spiritual blessing are in Him for He is the perfect image of God; in all that He is, says and does He shines out with God's glory (Hebrews 1:3).

Now give thanks to the God and Father of our Lord Jesus Christ! For in your union with Him, He has blessed you with every spiritual blessing by giving you the Holy Spirit (Ephesians 1:3).

You see the Father does not want you to fall short in any gift to express His Life and love, for there is a whole world around you who needs Him (1 Corinthians 1:4-7).

For Jesus, the gifts of the Holy Spirit revealed His Life with the Father and He came so all may have this Life (John 10:10).

Dear child of God, the wonders of the gifts of the Holy Spirit are immeasurably great when they bring glory to God. To see precious souls reconciled to the Father, worshipping Him in spirit and truth because of the Life they received is what satisfied Jesus (John 4:23-24, 34). When you consider this you will understand what Jesus meant when He said, 'It is more blessed to give than to receive' (Acts 20:35).

While there are many gifts of the Holy Spirit, they all serve Jesus in glorifying the Father.

Jesus said, 'I am telling you the truth: whoever believes in Me will do what I do — yes, he will do even greater things, because I am going to the Father. And I will do whatever you ask for in

My name, so that the Father's glory will be shown through the Son' (John 14:12-13 TEV).

Can you see that the gifts of the Holy Spirit will bring great glory to the Father when they reveal the Life Jesus has with Him in you?

Let's pray: Heavenly Father, I thank You for the grace You give through the Life Jesus has with You. You have enriched me through my union with Jesus with every gift of the Holy Spirit so that I may minister Your Life and love.

In Jesus' Name, Amen.

There are diversities of gifts, but the same Spirit
1 Corinthians 12:4

The Holy Spirit is the same yesterday, today and forever. He who hovered over the face of the waters at creation (Genesis 1:2) is the same Spirit who alighted upon Jesus in bodily form like a dove, when the Father said, 'You are my beloved Son; in whom I am well pleased' (Luke 3:22).

In Jesus you can perfectly see the Holy Spirit, as He is the Word made flesh.

Everything foretold by the Holy Spirit in Scripture was fulfilled in Jesus. The Holy Spirit spoke in detail of Jesus' birth, His Life, His death, His resurrection and the glory that would follow (Isaiah 7:14, 53; Psalm16; 1 Peter 1:11). Yes, the Life Jesus lived testified to the truth of the Holy Spirit.

When He was asked how He drove out an evil spirit, Jesus emphasized the importance of knowing the Holy Spirit because the sin never to be forgiven has its origin in misjudging Him (Matthew 12:32).

The Apostle Peter, filled with the Holy Spirit, said, 'This is what was spoken by the prophet Joel: And it shall come to pass in the last days, says God, that I will pour out of my Spirit on all flesh' (Acts 2:16-17).

Now this same Holy Spirit you see in Jesus is living in your heart; through Him you are blessed with every good and perfect gift that comes from the Father. He will teach you all things; He is the Truth, and as He has taught you so He will teach you to abide in Jesus Christ forever (1 John 2:27).

Yes, dear child of God, there are many gifts that come from the Life Jesus has with the Father, but it is the same Holy Spirit who takes 'what is mine,' as Jesus said, 'and declares it to you' (John 16:14).

So be encouraged, for the gifts will keep coming, for the Father longs to be glorified through His Son in you (John 14:13).

Let's pray: Heavenly Father, teach me to know and love the Holy Spirit. I open my heart to the gifts of the Holy Spirit so You may be glorified through Your Son in me.

In Jesus' Name, Amen.

But the manifestation of the Spirit is given to each one for the profit of all

1 Corinthians 12:6-7

When one is blessed with the Holy Spirit all are blessed. This is the gospel of Jesus; He being exalted to the right hand of God, and having received from the Father the promise of the Holy Spirit, poured out this which you now see and hear (Acts 2:33).

Think about it, 'Out of the fullness of the Life of this one Man Jesus we have all received [all had a share and we were all supplied with] one grace after another and spiritual blessing upon spiritual blessing and even favour upon favour and gift [heaped] upon gift' (John 1:16 AMPB).

Jesus understands that the Life He has with the Father is His so that He may give this same Life to all who come into the world (John 1:9).

When Jesus spoke the words of this Life, God bore witness with both signs and wonders, with various miracles, and gifts of the Holy Spirit, according to His own will (Hebrews 2:4).

In the same way, you are a witness of this Life and God Himself will bear witness of His Life in you by the gifts of the Holy Spirit.

So give thanks for the grace of God which was given to you by Christ Jesus, that you were enriched in everything by Him in all utterance and all knowledge, even as the testimony of Christ is confirmed in you, so that you come short in no gift, eagerly waiting for the revelation of our Lord Jesus Christ, who will also confirm you to the end, that you may be blameless in the day of our Lord Jesus Christ. God is faithful, by whom you were called into the fellowship of His Son, Jesus Christ our Lord (1 Corinthians 1:4-9).

Let's pray: Heavenly Father, I know all that I am and all that I have comes from You. Thank You for making me a witness of the Life Jesus has with You by the Holy Spirit. I trust You to convince those who hear me that this Life comes from You by the gifts of the Holy Spirit.

In Jesus' Name, Amen.

But one and the same Spirit works all these things, distributing to each one individually as He wills

1 Corinthians 12:11

Even as the human body has many parts which do not all have the same function, but work as one, so the Holy Spirit distributes the gifts to each one for the benefit of all.

It is important you look at this from Jesus' perspective, for in Him, His body, the Church is joined together. It is through His Life in you that Jesus joins you to others (Ephesians 3:18; 4:16). Jesus said, 'I am the vine, you are the branches. Abide in me, and I in you, for without Me you can do nothing' (John 15:5).

The Holy Spirit is the same and yet the way that His gifts function in one can be very different from the way His gifts function in another. However, now our differences have become our strength because we are one in Jesus.

The Bible compares this to the way the eye, the hand and feet all work as one in the body, while at the same time having completely different functions (1 Corinthians 12:14-18).

Jesus prayed, 'As You, Father, are in Me, and I in You; may they also be one in us. I in them, and You in Me; that they may be made perfect in oneness, and that the world may know that You have sent Me, and have loved them as You have loved Me' (John 17:21-23).

The power of this oneness by which we are joined is no less than what you see in Jesus and the Father. This oneness is the power of His Life at work in every one of us (Ephesians 4:16). As Jesus joins us together in Him, the gifts reach their ultimate purpose, to show the world the Father sent Jesus and loves us as He loves Him.

You see the gifts the Father gave Jesus revealed that the Life He lived came from Him. These same gifts He now gives reveal that the Life you live comes from Him.

Oh, how it pleases the Father to see His Life in you!

Now you who love Jesus even as you have received Him, receive one another, submit to one another and God, who gives patience and encouragement, will help you live in complete harmony with each other — each with the attitude of Jesus toward the other. Then all of you can join together with one voice, giving praise and glory to God, the Father of our Lord Jesus Christ (1 Peter 5:5; Romans 15:5-7 LB).

Let's pray: Heavenly Father, I give myself to You in the power of Your Life in me. I trust You to make me one with others so the world may know You sent Jesus and love me as You love Him.

In Jesus' Name, Amen.

For to one is given the word of wisdom through the Spirit, to another the word of knowledge through the same Spirit, to another faith by the same Spirit, to another gifts of healings by the same Spirit, to another the working of miracles, to another prophecy, to another discerning of spirits, to another different kinds of tongues, to another the interpretation of tongues

1 Corinthians 12:8-10

Jesus has been made wisdom to us (1 Corinthians 1.30). For God in His wisdom made it impossible for people to know Him by means of their own wisdom (1 Corinthians 1.21). Now this is the gift of wisdom – to be able to acknowledge God not just within yourself but in others. Samuel was given this gift of wisdom when He was sent to anoint David as king (1 Samuel 16:12-13). Ananias was gifted with wisdom when Jesus sent him to minister to Paul (Acts 9:10-19).

You may have all knowledge but the gift of the word of knowledge is to know what God knows – 'You are the Christ, the Son of the living God.' Jesus said, 'This gift of knowledge did not come from man but My Father who is in heaven' (Matthew 16:16-17).

You believe there is a God. Even the demons believe that and tremble, (James 2:19) but that is not the Holy Spirit's gift of faith. The Holy Spirit will give you the faith that comes straight from the heart of Jesus (Acts 3:16). His faith fills your heart with the wonders of the ever-living Word, empowering your whole being. Even so, the gifts of healing flow from the wounds of Jesus; they are most precious because there is no infirmity so strong Jesus cannot cure. As it is written in Isaiah 53, 'By His stripes you are healed!' The miracles Philip performed in Samaria proved that the message he spoke about Jesus was true (Acts 8:5-6).

Every gift of prophecy given by the Holy Spirit bears witness to Jesus and is intended to cause man's hearts to worship God, for the testimony of Jesus is the true spirit of prophecy (Revelation 19:10).

There are many spirits in this world, but not all are of God; the Holy Spirit will enable you to discern them for if they are of God they will acknowledge Jesus is the Christ, the Son of the living God (1 John 4:1-3).

Oh, the beauty of the gift of speaking in different kinds of tongues. Remember on the day of Pentecost how one hundred and twenty precious souls all were speaking in tongues, one could not hear what the other was saying except those who were outside, to whom the Holy Spirit gave the gift of interpretation as they heard them speaking in their own language of the wonderful works of God. This same gift of tongues convinced Peter that Cornelius' house had received the same Holy Spirit as he did on Pentecost (Acts 10:44-47).

Dear child of God, all these gifts of the Spirit come out of the Life Jesus has with the Father.

Let's pray: Heavenly Father, Your gifts are wonderful; I embrace them within myself and others. I trust You that I shall come short in no gift but that the testimony of Jesus will be confirmed in me.
In Jesus' Name, Amen.

There are differences of ministries, but the same Lord
1 Corinthians 12:5

Joshua was anointed with the Spirit that was upon Moses, and while the power that emanated from him was recognised as similar to that of Moses, his ministry was unique to his personality and God-given work (Numbers 27:18-20; Deuteronomy 34:9).

Elisha wore the robe of Elijah and was given a double portion of the Spirit that was upon Elijah (2 Kings 2:9-15).

What stands out in these examples is that God, who had established His authority in both Moses and Elijah, was able to equip Joshua and Elisha for the ministry through Moses and Elijah.

Now God has established all power and authority in heaven and earth in His Son Jesus, who when He ascended to the throne, gave His authority and power for some to be apostles, some prophets, some evangelists, and some pastors and teachers to equip the saints for the work of ministry (Ephesians 4:11).

Jesus said, 'All authority has been given to me in heaven and on earth. Go therefore and make disciples of all nations, baptising them, teaching them and lo, I am with you always, even to the end of the age' (Matthew 28:18-20).

Peter became a fisher of men because he believed Jesus. He later demonstrated Jesus' power and authority when he and John healed a lame man. When everyone ran after them, he said, 'Why look so intently at us, as though by our own power or godliness we had made this man walk? The God of our fathers glorified His Servant Jesus, whom He raised from the dead, of which we are witnesses. And His name, through faith in His name, has made this man strong, whom you see and know. Yes, the faith which comes through Him has given him this perfect soundness in the presence of you all' (Acts 3:12-16).

Peter was not Jesus, and yet he ministered in His power and authority.

The same is true for you; you can serve Jesus by ministering to others in His name and, like Peter and John, you will experience His power and authority.

Let's pray: Heavenly Father, I do not seek to establish my own name or ministry for You have established all Your power and authority in Jesus. Father, I long to serve You in the more excellent ministry of Jesus.

In Jesus' Name, Amen.

But now He has obtained a more excellent ministry, inasmuch as He is also mediator of a better covenant, which was established on better promises

Hebrews 8:6

The apostles began to speak from the Scriptures when they were filled with the Holy Spirit. This is exactly what they had seen in Jesus; when He spoke, what was written came alive, was powerful, active and fulfilled in their hearing (Luke 4:18-21).

Peter, filled with the Holy Spirit, touched the hearts of thousands of people when he said, 'This is what was spoken by the prophet Joel: 'And it shall come to pass in the last days, says God, that I will pour out my Spirit on all flesh' (Acts 2:16-17). You see, long ago God spoke in many different ways through the prophets [in visions, dreams, and even face to face], telling them little by little about His plans. But now in these days He has spoken to us through His Son to whom He has given everything and through whom He made the world and everything there is (Hebrews 1:1-2 LB).

Peter was inspired by the Holy Spirit when he spoke of the death and resurrection of Jesus, quoting Psalm 16: 'For You will not leave my soul in Hades, nor will You allow Your Holy One to see corruption. You have made known to me the ways of life; You will make me full of joy in Your presence' (Acts 2:28-33).

When everyone heard him speak God's Word, they were struck to the heart and became convicted and convinced that this Jesus, who had died was now made alive and exalted to the right hand of God. Having received from the Father the promised Holy Spirit, He poured out that which they had now seen and heard.

In Peter, you can clearly see the more excellent ministry of Jesus, as God worked with him, confirming what he said about Jesus by giving the Holy Spirit to all who believed.

Every ministry is given fruit to identify its origin. The more excellent ministry of Jesus gives fruit to eternal Life by washing away every sin and giving a new birth into the Life He has with the Father - a Life of righteousness, peace and joy in the Holy Spirit.

Now believe the Life you live is the ministry of Jesus. Believe God's Word is alive in you and believe the Father will bear witness to His Life in you by giving the Holy Spirit.

Let's pray: Heavenly Father, I long for the more excellent ministry of Jesus. Thank You for bearing witness to Your Son in me by giving the Holy Spirit.

In Jesus' Name, Amen.

---

*But rise and stand on your feet; for I have appeared to you for
this purpose, to make you a minister and a witness both of the
things which you have seen and of the things which I will yet
reveal to you*

Acts 26:16

Fundamentally, you need a personal relationship with Jesus to
have a ministry.

While there are many things that may motivate you to be in
ministry, there is nothing or no one who can keep your heart right
except Jesus.

It was the love of Jesus that compelled the Apostle Paul in the
ministry for which he worked so hard every day and often ended
up in jail. He was whipped times without number, and faced death
again and again. Five different times the Jews gave him thirty-nine
lashes. Three times he was beaten with rods. Once he was stoned.
Three times he was shipwrecked. Once he spent a whole night and
a day adrift at sea. He travelled many weary miles, faced danger
from flooded rivers and from robbers, faced danger from his
own people, the Jews, as well as from the Gentiles. He faced
danger in the cities, in the deserts, and on the stormy seas. He
faced danger from men who claimed to be Christians, but were
not and lived with the weariness of sleepless nights. Often he was
hungry and thirsty; often he shivered with cold, without enough
clothing to keep him warm. Then, besides all this, his daily burden
of how the churches were getting along; who was weak without
him feeling that weakness? Who was led astray, and it did not
burden him (2 Corinthians 11:23-29 NLT).

The ministry of Jesus is glorious, powerful and a God-given
privilege, but it is not without challenges. Jesus said, 'Whoever

lives in Me and I in him bears much fruit. However, apart from Me [cut off from vital union with Me] you can do nothing' (John 15:5 AMPB).

So you see Jesus Himself must be the all-compelling force in ministry.

Paul said, 'My life is worth nothing unless I use it for doing the work assigned me by the Lord Jesus — the work of telling others the Good News about God's wonderful kindness and love' (Acts 20:24 NLT).

As long as you keep your eyes on Jesus, His grace will make you sufficient to minister His Life-giving Spirit.

Let's pray: Heavenly Father, my life is worth nothing unless I serve Jesus. Thank You for making me a minister of the Life-giving Spirit of the new covenant.

In Jesus' Name, Amen.

And He said to me, 'My grace is sufficient for you, for My strength is made perfect in weakness.' Therefore most gladly I will rather boast in my infirmities, that the power of Christ may rest upon me

2 Corinthians 12:8-9

Jesus said, 'My grace is sufficient for you!'

The discovery of this all-sufficient grace is what teaches you in life and ministry to depend upon His strength, no matter how weak you are.

Moses needed God's grace, not merely because of the depth of his weaknesses, but because of what God called him to foreshadow concerning what He would do in the future through Jesus. You see you are not just to look to Jesus for this grace because of your weaknesses, but more than that, because of what He longs to reveal in you. For Moses, God demanded nothing less than His glory to be the sufficiency of his ministry; anything less meant Moses fell short in representing God (Numbers 20:12-13).

Even though David was anointed king, (Psalm 89:20) he was often painfully aware of his weaknesses and shortcomings, but knew how to strengthen himself in the Lord by meditating on His Word and singing His praises.

Now behold the grace of God in Jesus, how as the Son of Man He wept with strong cries and many tears to the Father because of His intense desire to do His will. In everything Jesus suffered, He perfectly displayed the Holy Spirit and was revealed as the Son of God not only in nature but action, as He gave Himself to God, crying with a loud voice, 'Father! Into Your hands I place My spirit!' He said this and died (Luke 23:46; Hebrews 5:7-9).

By this one sacrifice of Himself, Jesus made provision for you to receive an inner cleansing from all the sinful acts that lead to spiritual death. Therefore, Jesus can give you today a conscience free from guilt to serve God in true holiness. This is what it means to minister in the Life-giving Spirit of the new covenant, which is the power of the Life Jesus has with the Father revealed in you.

Now let me say this again, the grace of Jesus Christ is sufficient, no matter how weak you are, to empower you to minister His Life-giving Spirit and wash away every sin through a new Life in the Holy Spirit (Titus. 3:4-7).

Let's pray: Heavenly Father, I believe Your grace is sufficient and that in my weaknesses Your strength is made perfect in order that I may minister the Life-giving Spirit of the new covenant.
In Jesus' Name, Amen.

And He said to me, 'My grace is sufficient for you, for My strength is made perfect in weakness.' Therefore most gladly I will rather boast in my infirmities, that the power of Christ may rest upon me

2 Corinthians 12:8-9

A minister of Jesus Christ is a minister of the Life-giving Spirit of the new covenant.

The old covenant could never give life because of the weakness of human nature, but now God gives eternal Life through the resurrection of Jesus Christ (Hebrews 7:18-19).

Jesus gave His blood for an everlasting covenant and became the mercy seat (our 'propitiation') as He sat down at God's right hand to give you the assurance of faith that God's promise to give eternal Life in Him is 'yes', and through His Spirit in you an everlasting resounding praise of 'amen, it is so!' (Romans 3:25; Hebrews 13:20).

Jesus is the mercy seat of God; He is His footstool (1 Chronicles 28:2; Matthew 12:36)! Let us therefore exalt the Lord our God, and worship at His footstool; He is holy (Psalm 99:5).

You see, the blood of Jesus is the purchase price that gives Jesus the right to give you the Life He has with the Father. Knowing that you were not redeemed with corruptible things, like silver or gold, from your aimless conduct received by tradition from your fathers, but with the precious blood of Christ, as of a lamb without blemish and without spot. He indeed was foreordained before the foundation of the world, but was manifest in these last times for you who through Him believe in God, who raised Him from the dead and gave Him glory, so that your faith and hope are in God (1 Peter 1:18-21).

Now that you believe in Jesus, you are not only the recipient of His Life but a minister of His Life. You now live by the power of Jesus Christ in and upon you. So to boast in your own strength, compare yourself or feel inferior to anyone, would be mere foolishness for you know that the Life you now live is not your own but a gift of God (Galatians 2:20).

Jesus in you is the ministry of the Life-giving Spirit of the new covenant.

Let's pray: Heavenly Father, thank You that through His blood Jesus has all the authority and power He needs to give me the Life He has with You, so that I may be a minister of the Life-giving Spirit of the new covenant.

In Jesus' Name, Amen.

Bless the Lord, O my soul; and all that is within me, bless His holy name!

Psalm 103:1

The ministry of the Life-giving Spirit of the new covenant is a ministry of the heart from which this Life-force of God flows (Proverbs 4:20). In Jesus you see the unhindered flow of the Life He has with the Father - a Life filled with the loving-kindness and truth of the Holy Spirit.

Jesus said, in a loud voice, 'If any man is thirsty; let him come to Me and drink!'

'He who believes in Me [who cleaves to and trusts in and relies on Me] as the Scripture has said, from his innermost being shall flow [continuously] springs and rivers of living water. But He was speaking here of the Spirit, whom those who believed (trusted, had faith) in Him were afterward to receive. For the [Holy] Spirit had not yet been given, because Jesus was not yet glorified (raised to honour)' (John 7:37-39 AMPB).

In April of 1918, during World War 1, Duncan Campbell was carried from the battlefield into a medical station. As he lay wounded, Campbell prayed the prayer of Robert Murray M'Cheyne: 'Lord, make me as holy as a saved sinner can be.' As the Holy Spirit's purifying presence flooded Campbell's soul, he cried out in the Gaelic language, 'Bless the Lord, O my soul and all that is within me, bless His holy name.' Soon seven Canadian soldiers lying nearby were glorious saved. This life-changing experience propelled Campbell into a lifetime of ministering the Life-giving Spirit of Jesus Christ. When Campbell returned home God used him mightily to bring revival to the Hebrides. When Campbell preached about Jesus the power of His Life was so great that a whole village of six hundred people gave their hearts to Jesus and were gloriously filled with the Holy Spirit.

Dear child of God, there is no greater ministry than the Life-giving Spirit of the new covenant flowing from your heart, professing, 'Jesus is Lord, for God has highly exalted Him and given Him the name which is above every name, that at the name of Jesus every knee should bow, of those in heaven, and of those on earth, and of those under the earth, and that every tongue should confess that Jesus Christ is Lord, to the glory of God the Father' (Philippians 2:9-11).

Let's pray: Heavenly Father, make me as holy as a saved sinner can be! I am thirsty for the river of Your Life to flow from my heart so that I may speak in the name of Jesus and see Your power unto salvation.

In Jesus' Name, Amen.

*To reveal His Son in me, that I might preach Him among the
Gentiles, I did not immediately confer with flesh and blood*
Galatians 1:16

In Jesus you receive the Life-giving Spirit of the New Covenant!
The ministry of this Life-giving Spirit starts, is upheld, and made
perfect through the joy of the Father revealing His Son, Jesus
Christ in you.

Robert Murray M'Cheyne said, 'I am persuaded that I shall obtain
the highest amount of present happiness, I shall do the most for
God's glory and the good of man, and I shall have the fullest
reward in eternity, by maintaining a conscience always washed
in Christ's blood, by being filled with the Holy Spirit at all times,
and by attaining the most entire likeness to Christ in mind,
will, and heart, that is possible for a redeemed sinner to attain
to in this world.'

M'Cheyne also said, 'I am persuaded to be fully conformed to
the image of Jesus in all things and that whenever anyone from
without or my own heart from within or any circumstance
contradicts this it is the voice of the devil, God's enemy, the
enemy of my soul, and of all good - the most foolish, wicked,
and miserable of all the creatures.'

Robert M'Cheyne was still very young when the Life Jesus has
with the Father gained such influence upon his soul. His life,
ministry and prayers set men like Duncan Campbell and countless
others on fire with a holy zeal for Jesus. While all these men served
God in their generation it is now your turn to bear the torch of
the Life-giving Spirit of Jesus Christ.

Therefore, let the thoughts of Robert M'Cheyne inspire you to pray daily, for the Father longs to reveal His Son in you so that in all you are, say and do Jesus is revealed.

Let's pray: Heavenly Father, how I love You for revealing Your Son in me! I know I am being renewed in the inward man daily so that in all I am, say and do Jesus is revealed.

In Jesus' Name, Amen.

To them God willed to make known what are the riches of the
glory of this mystery among the Gentiles: which is Christ in you,
the hope of glory

Colossians 1:27

It was the will of God in the men and women of past generations
which gave them such force to achieve so much for His glory and
for the good of man.

The truly circumcised heart that has been made alive with Jesus is
born of God and lives by the same godly fear and loving nature
you see in Jesus (Matthew 26:39; Hebrews 5:7-9).

You see this is the will of your Father who is in heaven, that
through Christ in you others may come to know the glory of the
Life that awaits them in His presence.

There is no greater joy than the joy you will experience when you
see Jesus and delight in His presence together with all those who
believe in Him through your testimony (1 Thessalonians 2:19-20).

I had just celebrated my eighteenth birthday when Jesus called me
into His service. While I was singing with all my heart in gratitude
for the blood that Jesus shed for me, I had a vision and saw myself
walking into heaven; the light that shone upon me was the Life of
Christ. As I looked around me I saw many people standing in
darkness, who were not going with me, so I began to cry, 'No,
Lord Jesus, I don't want to go to heaven alone!'

Jesus said, 'Let not your heart be troubled; you believe in God,
believe also in Me. In My Father's house are many mansions; if it
were not so, I would have told you. I go to prepare a place for
you. I will come again and receive you to Myself; that where I am,
there you may be also. And where I go you know, and the way you

know. I am the way, the truth, and the life. No one comes to the Father except through Me' (John 14:1-6).

This is the will of God, that none should perish but all come to Him through Jesus Christ (1 Timothy 2:3-6).

I charge you therefore, by the will of God, to pursue every opportunity to present Jesus and make Him known in the power of the Holy Spirit, for so the Father will give you eternal fruit for His glory in the precious souls who will be saved because of your testimony.

Oh, what joy when we will all stand before His throne in glory!

Let's pray: Heavenly Father, let Your will be done in me as it is in heaven. I ask You to give me more fruit for the glory of Your name. I pray to see precious souls saved.

In Jesus' Name, Amen.

Him we preach, warning every man and teaching every man in
all wisdom, that we may present every man perfect in Christ Jesus
Colossians 1:28

It was none other than the revelation of Jesus that made Paul
effective and enduring as an apostle. Toward the end of his
life, when Paul stood before King Agrippa sharing his testimony
about Jesus, he said, 'I was not disobedient to the heavenly vision'
(Acts 26:19).

You see the Holy Spirit was constantly filling Paul with the
knowledge of the Father in the Son. Paul knew through the Life of
Jesus in him that he was made perfectly welcome, holy, acceptable
and well-pleasing to the Father (Ephesians 1:4). So the riches of
the glory of the Life Jesus has with the Father were not only the
joy of Paul's salvation but his ministry.

Dear child of God, let this wonderful liberating truth deeply
penetrate your heart - that the purpose of ministry is to see the
Life Jesus has with the Father formed in you. For when you have
Jesus, you have everything He has with the Father.

Paul's vision of Jesus empowered him to reach the people of his
day and open their eyes, in order to turn them from darkness to
light, and from the power of Satan to God, that they may receive
forgiveness of sins and an inheritance among those who are
sanctified by faith in Jesus (Acts 26:18).

It is glorious and most wonderful to make Jesus known in the
power of the Holy Spirit, for in Him lie hidden all the mighty
treasures of God. Therefore, delight yourself in Jesus, for even
as you trusted Him to save you, trust Him too for each day's
problems; live in vital union with Him. Let your roots grow down

into Him and draw your nourishment from your union with Him. See that you keep on growing in the Lord, and become strong and vigorous in Him. Let your life overflow with joy and thanksgiving for all He has done. For in Jesus there is all of God in a human body; so you have everything when you have Him, and you are filled with God through your union with Jesus Christ (Colossians 2:3-10 LB).

Let's pray: Heavenly Father, I know Your Holy Spirit is at work in me so that I may be perfect before You in Jesus. How I long to see Your Spirit work through me to present others perfect before You in Christ Jesus.

In Jesus' Name, Amen.

*For the law of the Spirit of life in Christ Jesus has made me free
from the law of sin and death*

Romans 8:2

By the commandments of the old covenant no one is saved
(Galatians 2:16) because through the knowledge of the law came
condemnation, not because the law is evil but because of the law
of sin and death (Romans 3:20).

You may delight yourself in the law of God day and night and yet
sink deeper and deeper in the mire of your own weak nature
crying, 'O, wretched man that I am! Who will deliver me?! For
what I am doing, I do not understand. For what I will to do, that
I do not practice; but what I hate, that I do. If then, I do what I
will not to do, I agree with the law that it is good. But now, it is
no longer I who do it, but sin that dwells in me. For I know that
in me (that is, in my flesh) nothing good dwells; for to will is
present with me, but how to perform what is good I do not find'
(Romans 7:24, 14-18).

You see this is why God called you to be a minister of the law of
the Spirit of Life in Christ Jesus, because the Life Jesus has with
the Father knows no sin. To minister the letter of the law without
the Spirit of Life in Christ brings forth death.

To minister the Life of Jesus flowing from your heart like a river
will fill people with the joy of what they are freely receiving in
Christ - a Life that knows no sin, no condemnation, no separation
but only perfect righteousness, peace and joy in the Holy Spirit.

The Gospel of Jesus is good news!

Pray for the good news to reach people through you now that the
Holy Spirit is revealing the riches of the glory of the Life Jesus has
with the Father in you.

Dear child of God, you have bread to spare, for the Life-giving Spirit of Jesus in you is the Bread of Life and Jesus is asking you to share your bread with the hungry!

Let's pray: Heavenly Father, I know You are upholding me through the law of the Spirit of Life in Christ Jesus so that I may live in sweet fellowship with You and share Your Life and love with the next person I meet.

In Jesus' Name, Amen.

But that is why God had mercy on me, so that Christ Jesus could use me as a prime example of His great patience with even the worst sinners. Then others will realise that they, too, can believe in Him and receive eternal life

1 Timothy 1:16 (NLT)

The Life Jesus lived in the body gave light for everyone to know and find the only true living God (1 John 5:20). For it pleased the Father that in Him, the Son of Man, the fullness of Himself would be manifest (Colossians 2:9). This is why Jesus said, 'He who has seen Me has seen the Father, for I am in the Father, and the Father is in Me' (John 14:9-11).

Can you see the grace and glory of the Life Jesus has with the Father? For this, dear child of God, is what He now gives to you so abundantly that it will flow from you like a river.

You know those who are without Jesus live on earth like in a dry and thirsty land where there is no water. But the Life you live is like living water to quench their thirst for Life.

The Apostle Paul was transformed when he met Jesus. How could Jesus give him His Life after all he had done against Him? But Jesus, filled with faith and love for Paul, made him an example of what He can do for you.

Can you, like Paul, see the grace of Jesus that He continuously gives you His Life? Do you realise the Life you now live is not your own but a gift of God and that you have become an example of what Jesus can do for others?

This is what Jesus meant when He said, 'Let your light so shine before men, that they may see your good works and glorify your Father in heaven' (Matthew 5:16).

Therefore, as beloved children of God full of the Life, the faith and love of Jesus, realise that the message of Christ's Life is shining from you. For now God can always point to you as an example of how very, very rich His kindness is, as shown in all He has done for you through Jesus Christ (Ephesians 2:7 LB).

Let's pray: Heavenly Father, how great is Your grace that I may share the Life Jesus has with You. I love being an example of Your great love.

In Jesus' Name, Amen.

That the sharing of your faith may become effective by the acknowledgment of every good thing which is in you in Christ Jesus

Philemon 6

A minister of the Lord Jesus must live ready to bring forth out of the rich treasure of his heart the Life-giving Spirit of Jesus Christ.

All through Scripture God tells you to seek Him and love Him with your whole heart and to keep your heart with all diligence because it is the wellspring from which Life flows.

Jesus spoke of this when He said to the woman at the well, 'If you knew the gift God has for you, you would ask Me and I would give you Life-giving water so you would never thirst again. The Life I give will become like a fountain springing up in you with everlasting Life' (John 4).

Dearly loved child of God, Jesus is calling you to come and drink deeply from the Life He has with the Father. When you daily seek to quench your thirst for living in intimacy with Jesus you will never thirst again for His Life in you is the wellspring of Life.

A well trained mind is stayed on God by meditating on His Word, but this will only prepare the channel through which the Life flows. Your heart needs communion with the Father and the Son in Holy Spirit-filled prayer. There is no substitute for prayer to prepare the heart! Jesus often prayed before morning light as well as all night. He lived in unbroken fellowship with the Father and it was from this intimate fellowship that all the unlimited blessings flowed.

You can clearly see the Life Jesus has with the Father by the Life-giving words He spoke.

Now this Life-giving ministry you see in Jesus is what the Father is pleased to reveal in you as you live in fellowship with Jesus.

Jesus said, 'The same works I do, you will do also' (John 14:12). What the Father started in Jesus, He wants to continue in you!

Let's pray: Heavenly Father, I love You with my whole heart, mind, soul and body. Thank You for revealing the Life-giving ministry of Jesus in me.

In Jesus' Name, Amen.

That is, that God was in Christ reconciling the world to Himself,
not imputing their trespasses to them, and has committed to us
the word of reconciliation

2 Corinthians 5:19

This makes you want to shout and sing 'Hallelujah' together
with the great multitude which no one can number of all nations,
tribes, peoples, and tongues, standing before the throne and
before the Lamb, clothed with white robes, with palm branches
in their hands, and crying out with a loud voice, saying 'Salvation
belongs to our God who sits on the throne, and to the Lamb!'
(Revelation 7:9-10).

What a privilege to join the great cloud of witnesses around
the throne and become a minister of the Life Jesus has with the
Father! The ministry of reconciliation has the power not to
impute trespasses but take away all sense of shame, blame, guilt
and condemnation by empowering all who receive Jesus with His
Life of perfect righteousness, peace and joy in the Holy Spirit.

This is the wonder of the Life-giving Spirit of the new covenant;
we are given the power to reconcile all who receive Jesus to the
Father (John 1:12). Only through being one with Jesus can we
ever live free from sin and enjoy the Life He has with the Father.

There is no salvation outside of Jesus, for there is no other name
under heaven given unto men by which we must be saved! Jesus
said, 'I am the way, the truth, and the Life. No one comes to the
Father except through Me' (John 14:6).

Therefore, by the mercies of God and the mighty inward working
of the Holy Spirit, your life and ministry stands in reference to
Jesus who bore the pain and shame of all our sins in His own body

on the Cross. Jesus who knew no sin became sin for us as He bore the punishment of God's wrath and became the source of eternal salvation and reconciliation.

This is the power not to impute men their trespasses but freely impart the righteousness, peace and joy Jesus has with the Father.

Now this is the riches of the glory of His grace, to live in the continual supply of His Life.

Let's pray: Heavenly Father, I give myself to serve You in the ministry of reconciliation by not imputing trespasses to men but freely imparting the righteousness, peace and joy Jesus has with You in heaven.

In Jesus' Name, Amen.

Blessed is he whose transgression is forgiven, whose sin is covered. Blessed is the man to whom the Lord does not impute iniquity, and in whose spirit there is no deceit

Psalm 32:1-2

The misery of living in sin seems to have no end when you see the evil in this world. But this is exactly why Jesus came, as it is written, 'For there is born to you this day in the city of David a Saviour, who is Christ the Lord and you shall call His name Jesus, for He will save His people from their sins' (Luke 2:11; Matthew 1:21).

When the Apostle Peter was learning from Jesus how He as Saviour of the world dealt with sin, he asked, 'Lord, how often shall my brother sin against me, and I forgive him?' Up to seven times?' Jesus said to him, 'I do not say to you, up to seven times, but up to seventy times seven.' Then Jesus shared a story of a man who owed ten thousand talents to teach Peter what He meant. Jesus said the man was not able to pay, so his master commanded that he be sold, with his wife and children and all that he had, and that payment be made. But the servant fell down before him, saying, 'Master, have patience with me, and I will pay you all.' Then the master of that servant was moved with compassion, released him, and forgave him the debt.

Unless like Peter you learn from Jesus how to deal with sin, you will always stumble at the offensiveness of sin and fail to minister effectively the Life-giving Spirit of the new covenant.

You see in the days of Peter, one denarius was a day's wage (Matthew 20:2) and there were about ten thousand denarii in one talent. Jesus said that the man owed ten thousand talents, so if he had worked every day of the year it would take him 273,972 years to pay his debt! We may not always realise that we are unable to repay the debt of sin, so to begin to count how often to forgive shows you need a revelation of the price Jesus paid in shedding His blood.

In the ministry of the new covenant the power to forgive and cleanse is phenomenal and continually sufficient to conquer sin (1 John 1:9). But there is more, for His Life with the Father gives power for anyone who receives Him to live free from sin and be transformed into His likeness.

Begin to sing, 'Would you be free from your burden of sin? There is power in the blood...there is power, power wonder working power in the precious blood of the Lamb.'

Let's pray: Heavenly Father, teach me out of the riches of Your grace never to fail to minister Your forgiveness.

In Jesus' Name, Amen.

Would you be free from the burden of sin?
There's power in the blood, power in the blood;
Would you o'er evil a victory win?
There's wonderful power in the blood.

Refrain:
There is power, power, wonder working power
In the blood of the Lamb;
There is power, power, wonder working power In the
precious blood of the Lamb.

Would you be free from your passion and pride?
There's power in the blood, power in the blood;
Come for a cleansing to Calvary's tide;
There's wonderful power in the blood.

Would you be whiter, much whiter than snow?
There's power in the blood, power in the blood;
Sin stains are lost in its life giving flow.
There's wonderful power in the blood.

Would you do service for Jesus your King?
There's power in the blood, power in the blood;
Would you live daily His praises to sing?
There's wonderful power in the blood.

Lewis E. Jones, 1899.

Or do you despise the riches of His goodness, forbearance, and longsuffering, not knowing that the goodness of God leads you to repentance?

Romans 2:4

Jesus said 'I have not come to call the righteous, but sinners, to repentance' (Luke 5:32).

In one of His parables, Jesus described a father with two sons of which the younger asked for his inheritance. Not many days after, his son gathered all together, journeyed to a far country, and there wasted his possessions with prodigal living. But when he had spent all, there arose a severe famine in that land and he began to be in want. Then he came to himself and said, 'How many of my father's hired servants have bread enough and to spare, and I perish with hunger? I will arise and go to my father, and will say to him, 'Father, I have sinned against heaven and before you, and I am no longer worthy to be called your son. Make me like one of your hired servants.' He arose and came to his father. But when he was still a great way off, his father saw him and had compassion, and ran and fell on his neck and kissed him' (Luke 15:12-19).

You see Jesus came to reveal the love of the Father. He came so that repentance and remission of sins should be preached in His name to all nations (Luke 24:47). God has exalted Jesus to His right hand to be Prince and Saviour, to give repentance and forgiveness of sins. And you are His witnesses to these things, and so also is the Holy Spirit whom God has given to those who obey Him (Acts 5:31-32).

The Heavenly Father will continually compel you with His love to be full of the riches of His goodness, forbearance and longsuffering so that you may open people's eyes, in order to turn them from darkness to light and from the power of Satan to God - that they may receive forgiveness of sins and an inheritance among those who are sanctified by faith in Jesus (Acts 26:18).

Remember, a servant of the Lord Jesus must not quarrel but be gentle to all, able to teach, patient, in humility correcting those who are in opposition, if God perhaps will grant them repentance, so that they may know the truth, and that they may come to their senses and escape the snare of the devil, having been taken captive by him to do his will (2 Timothy 2:24-26).

Let's pray: Heavenly Father, fill and flood my heart continually with Your goodness, forbearance and longsuffering so that I may open peoples' eyes and help them turn in repentance to You.

In Jesus' Name, Amen.

The Lord is not slack concerning His promise, as some count slackness, but is longsuffering toward us, not willing that any should perish but that all should come to repentance

2 Peter 3:8-9

It can be very difficult when you have to bear the unwillingness of others to turn to God.

Ever since your heart was filled with faith, you have known all it takes is to call on the name of Jesus to be saved. But how then shall they call on Him in whom they have not believed? And how shall they believe in Him of whom they have not heard? And how shall they hear without a preacher? And how shall they preach unless they are sent? As it is written: 'How beautiful are the feet of those who preach the gospel of peace, who bring glad tidings of good things!' (Romans 10:14-15).

You see, God is not willing that anyone should perish but that all may hear the good news, call on the name of Jesus and be saved.

Could it be, while you are waiting for someone to turn to God, that He is waiting for you to share His love with them? The Apostle Paul said, 'My life is worth nothing unless I use it for doing the work assigned me by the Lord Jesus — the work of telling others the Good News about God's wonderful kindness and love' (Acts 20:24 NLT).

Life on earth can seem meaningless until the joy of heaven floods your soul as you see someone turn to Jesus Christ as their Lord and Saviour. Jesus said, 'I say to you there will be more joy in heaven over one sinner who repents than over ninety-nine just persons who need no repentance' (Luke 15:7).

William Booth wrote in 1879, 'We are salvation people - this is our speciality - getting people saved and keeping them saved.

Look at this! Clear your vision! Halt, stand still and afresh and more fully apprehend and comprehend your calling. You are working together with God for the salvation of your fellow men. What is your business in life? Not merely to save your soul and make yourself meet for paradise?

Rescue the perishing. There they are all around you everywhere, crowd upon crowds, multitudes. Be skilled. Improve yourself. Study your business. Be self-sacrificing. Remember your Master. What you lose for His sake, and for the sake of poor souls for whom He died, you shall find again. Stick to it! Having put your hand to the Gospel plough, don't look back.'

Let's pray: Heavenly Father, fill my heart afresh with the fire of Your love for the precious souls for whom Jesus died. I believe You want all men to be saved through faith.

In Jesus' Name, Amen.

For this is good and acceptable in the sight of God our Saviour, who desires all men to be saved and to come to the knowledge of the truth. For there is one God and one mediator between God and men, the man Christ Jesus, who gave Himself a ransom for all, to be testified in due time

1 Timothy 2:3-6

William Booth truly caught the fire of God's desire for all men to be saved!

There is no question as to God's mandate for your life in Christ Jesus; He said, 'For God so loved the world that He gave His only begotten Son, that whoever believes in Him should not perish but have everlasting life. For God did not send His Son into the world to condemn the world, but that the world through Him might be saved' (John 3:16-17).

You see everyone needs Jesus. He is the only Saviour of the world. He is the only mediator between God and men; the only one who gave Himself a ransom for all; and He is able to save to the uttermost all who call upon His name.

Let this good news deeply penetrate your heart, for there is no guessing as to the urgency of the emergency of lost souls when the cross of Jesus has been sounding the alarm for the last two thousand years for all to be saved.

If you heard a fire alarm, you would want everyone in danger to escape wouldn't you?

Let therefore your heart be set on fire with God's desire to sound the alarm and tell the world about Jesus, for your life stands in reference to the cross where He died for the sins of all mankind.

Jesus who died has risen! He ascended to the Father and is pouring out His Spirit on all flesh; this is what you want to tell everyone, because you feel God's love for them.

I encourage you to read books such as 'Passion for Souls' and 'The Revival we Need' by Oswald J. Smith. His works have inspired men like Billy Graham and many others to do something good for the world.

Keep telling people about the love of Jesus for them and His sacrifice on the cross, His death and resurrection, His going to the Father and sending the Holy Spirit. Why? Because this is His commission for you; it is your reason for living.

You can do something to save the world by telling them about Jesus!

Let's pray: Heavenly Father, thank You for making me a witness of Jesus and giving me Your power through the gospel to do something to save the world.

In Jesus' Name, Amen.

Therefore, brethren, seek out from among you seven men of good reputation, full of the Holy Spirit and wisdom, whom we may appoint over this business; but we will give ourselves continually to prayer and to the ministry of the word

Acts 6:3-4

The men Jesus found whom He called to become His Apostles were given to Him by God (John 17:6).

You see, when God made these men one with Jesus they had a profound lasting effect on the world.

It was not their education or training that made them so effective, but Jesus (Acts 4:13)!

The Apostle Paul writes, 'For you see your calling, brethren, that not many wise according to the flesh, not many mighty, not many noble, are called. But God has chosen the foolish things of the world to put to shame the wise, and God has chosen the weak things of the world to put to shame the things which are mighty; and the base things of the world and the things which are despised God has chosen, and the things which are not, to bring to nothing the things that are, that no flesh should glory in His presence. But of Him you are in Christ Jesus, who became for us wisdom from God — and righteousness and sanctification and redemption — that, as it is written, 'He who glories, let him glory in the LORD" (1 Corinthians 1:26-31).

My father once said to me, 'Robert, don't be too concerned what you will do for God, just be sure He knows where to find you. Remember King David was but the least in his family - he took care of His father's sheep - but God found him!' As it is written, 'I have found David the son of Jesse, a man after My own heart,

350

who will do all My will. With My holy oil I have anointed him' (Acts 13:21-22; Psalm 89:20).

Consider how God found David tending his father's sheep - praying, singing and meditating on His Word, trusting God to give him victory over the lion and bear who sought to destroy the flock. Now God was able to make this man the shepherd of His people Israel. He loved him so much that He was pleased to be called, 'Son of David' (Matthew 21:9).

The same heart and mind you see in David is now also being formed in you through your union with Jesus Christ, so that you may be found by God in Christ - holy, acceptable and well-pleasing in His sight, ready for every good work in the power of the Holy Spirit.

You are the one God is looking for, full of the Holy Spirit and wisdom.

Let's pray: Heavenly Father, here I am in Your presence, lifting holy hands to You, singing praises to Jesus for making me a person after Your own heart who will do all Your will.

In Jesus' Name, Amen.

But when He saw the multitudes, He was moved with compassion for them, because they were weary and scattered, like sheep having no shepherd

Matthew 9:36

If you are to become a minister after God's own heart as Jesus was, then you will have to have a vision of His love for people.

When Jesus was asked how He was able to do what He did for people He said, 'Most assuredly, I say to you, the Son can do nothing of Himself, but what He sees the Father do; for whatever He does, the Son also does in like manner' (John 5:19).

When Jesus called me by His word in 1986 to go to Britain, I knew I was in His perfect will, so I obeyed His call. However the struggle to do His will was so great that it brought me to my knees for many hours every day.

One Saturday evening, a dear Pastor called and asked if I would come the following morning to share my vision for Britain. I agreed, but my deep sense of inability to do anything about the apparent need of some sixty million people overwhelmed me so much that I cried out in prayer to God all night, 'Father, I don't know what to do but my eye is on You!'

That night I had a vision, and saw multitudes of precious people and Jesus walking among them, healing them all. When I saw the love of Jesus I wept out loud.

Today this vision burns in me and compels me to live not for myself but for Him who loved me and gave Himself for me.

Dear child of God, this vision is for you too! Jesus said, 'The harvest truly is plentiful, but the labourers are few. Therefore pray the Lord of the harvest to send out labourers into His harvest'

(Matthew 9:37-38). As you pray, the Holy Spirit will fill you with the love of Jesus and His love will open your eyes to see the need of others.

Now look around you, because the anointing of Jesus in you is reaching out in love to restore precious souls to God and to heal them all.

Let's pray: Heavenly Father, open my eyes; I want to see Jesus, in His great love, saving and healing precious people through me.

In Jesus' Name, Amen.

Praise the Lord, my soul! All my being, praise His holy name! Praise the Lord, my soul, and do not forget how kind He is. He forgives all my sins and heals all my diseases
Psalm 103:1-3 (TEV)

Of all the good graces that come forth from the Life Jesus has with the Father, His steadfast love to always forgive is one of the greatest of them all. The reason Jesus has such all-sufficient power to forgive is because He now lives in the satisfaction of seeing the fruit of the travail of His soul in suffering for our sins. You see, Jesus reigns at the throne of God as the Lamb of God who takes away the sin of the world! (John 1:29) 'He shall see [the fruit] of the travail of His soul and be satisfied; by His knowledge of Himself [which He possesses and imparts to others] shall My [uncompromisingly] righteous One, My Servant, justify many *and* make many righteous (upright and in right standing with God), for He shall bear their iniquities *and* their guilt [with the consequences, says the Lord]' (Isaiah 53.11 AMPB).

John the beloved writes, '...and you know that He was manifested to take away our sins, and in Him there is no sin. Whoever abides in Him does not sin. Whoever sins has neither seen Him nor known Him' (1 John 3:6).

Dear child of God, these things are written to fill your heart with the light of the Life Jesus has with the Father, so you will not only live in the joy of complete forgiveness but also in the power of His sinless Life. Now He who always forgives is He who always heals all our diseases! Jesus said, 'Which is easier, to say, 'Your sins are forgiven you,' or to say, 'Arise and walk'? But that you may know that the Son of Man has power on earth to forgive sins.' Then He said to the paralytic, 'Arise, take up your bed, and go to your house.' And he arose and departed to his house' (Matthew 9:5-7).

Throughout Scripture we see that forgiveness and healing go hand in hand. Not that all sickness is a direct result of sin, but the same steadfast love that reveals God's glory to forgive also heals every disease.

Jeremiah said, 'Heal me, O Lord, and I shall be healed. Save me, and I shall be saved, for You are my praise' (Jeremiah 17:14).

Now if you are suffering with anything in your spirit, soul or body, look to Jesus who fills you with the knowledge of Himself in all His power to save and heal you!

Let's pray: Heavenly Father, I long to live in the knowledge of the power of Jesus to forgive and heal every disease. Father, You are my praise!

In Jesus' Name, Amen.

Do not be overcome by evil, but overcome evil with good
Romans 12:21

It is clear to see how Jesus, through the goodness of God in Him, went about doing good and healing all who were oppressed by the devil (Acts 10:38).

When Moses asked to see God's glory, God said, 'I will make all my goodness pass before you, and I will proclaim my name, THE LORD, before you; for I will be gracious to whom I will be gracious, and will show mercy and loving-kindness on whom I will show mercy and loving-kindness' (Exodus 33:19 AMPB).

In the ministry of the new covenant we are empowered to minister in the glorious goodness of the Life-giving Spirit of Jesus Christ whereby people are drawn to Him, and receive from Him until they are filled with the fullness of Him.

This ministry is the work of the Father. As Jesus said, 'No one can come to Me unless the Father who sent Me draws Him' (John 6:44).

You see, this is the goodness of God - to draw all people to Jesus.

In ministry anyone can be tempted to be merely mechanical and spend too much time polishing the method and not enough time seeking God to know that He is good.

We need to feed continually on God's goodness. 'Oh, taste and see that the Lord is good; blessed is the man who trusts in Him!' (Psalm 34:8).

Dear child of God, hear the Father speaking to you today when He says, 'Because he has set his love upon Me, therefore will

I deliver him; I will set him on high, because he knows and understands My name [has a personal knowledge of My mercy, love, and kindness — trusts and relies on Me, knowing I will never forsake him, no, never' (Psalm 91:14 AMPB).

This is where Jesus lived when He walked the earth, in complete victory over all evil; and this is where He is calling you to live in Him in the Life He has with the Father.

I pray you are being filled to overflowing with God's goodness!

Let's pray: Heavenly Father, my heart overflows with love for You, that You share Your own goodness and glory with me. I love living in fellowship with You in Jesus. You are so good to me! Your mercies never end.

In Jesus' Name, Amen.

As we know Jesus better, His divine power gives us everything we need for living a godly life. He has called us to receive His own glory and goodness!

2 Peter 1:3 (NLT)

When the Bible says, 'Oh, taste and see that the Lord is good', the invitation is not metaphorical but real and it is beyond your highest hopes and dreams. Moses was so filled with God's goodness that his face became radiant – so radiant in fact that the children of Israel could not bear to see the glory that was emanating from him. These things are in the Bible to inspire your expectations as you become a minister of the new covenant, which is nothing less than the ministry of the Life-giving Spirit of Jesus, of which Moses only received a glimpse (2 Corinthians 3:7).

If Moses only caught a glimpse of these things, how much more should we, who have the Life Jesus has with the Father in us, be radiant with the light of His Life, which is the ministry of the new covenant.

Now that we have been given this wonderful ministry by the mercies of God and are enabled by Him with spiritual gifts, we do not become discouraged, lose heart, or become despondent with fear and faint with weariness and exhaustion to the point of giving up.

We have renounced and shun every disgraceful way; for we refuse to deal craftily or to adulterate or handle dishonestly the Word of God, but we state the truth openly. And so we commend ourselves in the sight and presence of God to every man's conscience.

Dear child of God, let the glory and goodness of God fill and flood your life so that the Gospel may not be hidden and so that the knowledge of God may not be veiled by your human nature.

For now that you have become a partaker of the Life Jesus has with the Father, let your life shine forth with the light of His Life.

We know that the Gospel is veiled and hidden from those who are perishing because the god of this world has blinded their minds so that they cannot see the illuminating light of the Gospel of the glory of Jesus Christ.

Therefore we live for the Gospel to be unveiled in us and do not preach ourselves but Jesus Christ as Lord.

Let's pray: Heavenly Father, I long to live in the fullness of the stature of Jesus so all may see You in me. I have renounced every secret thought, feeling, desire and all underhandedness, method and art that would veil the Gospel in me. I pray that the light of Your Life shines bright in me for all to see.

In Jesus' Name, Amen.

But as we have been approved by God to be entrusted with the gospel, even so we speak, not as pleasing men, but God who tests our hearts

1 Thessalonians 2:4

God, who searches our hearts and deepest thoughts, knows our inclinations, intentions and motivations. Even when we are surrounded by the enemies of Jesus Christ it is clear for all to hear and see that we do not preach with any false motives or evil purposes in mind; for we are perfectly straightforward and sincere. We speak as messengers from God, trusted by Him to tell the truth. We do not change His message to suit the tastes of those who hear it, for we serve God alone, before whom our hearts are known. We would never try to win anyone with flattery. God knows we do not pretend to be anyone's friend so that they would give us money. As for the praise of man, we never ask for it, for God Himself fills our hearts with gratitude to represent His Son. His love for Jesus overwhelms us.

You see, this love of the Father for Jesus is what we feel for all His children. This is why we are gentle, kind and tender-hearted among God's people because we are constantly overcome by the Father's love for them.

Oh dear child of God, can you see the Father's love in Jesus when He gave His life for the church? This is why we love loving people so much that we give not only God's message but our own lives too.

The Gospel to us is therefore not some occupation for an income; on the contrary, it is God who meets our needs, for we desire to be a burden to no one. We pray that it is clear for all to see that the Father bears witnesses of His Son in us and that we live pure and undefiled lives - that we are honest, faultless and filled with His love.

We pray that the way we live our daily lives will not embarrass God but bring joy to Him.

We can't stop thanking God for the privilege of preaching the Gospel of Jesus Christ. His Life in us is the ever-living hope of glory. We know that the words we speak in making known the Gospel are not our own, but the very Word of God - which has changed our lives.

We are servants of Jesus Christ by the will of God!

Let's pray: Heavenly Father, it is perfect, right and so good to represent Jesus in the wonderful Life He has with You and all the blessings You give us in Him. I love You Father.

In Jesus' Name, Amen.

Everyone else is concerned only with his own affairs, not with the cause of Jesus Christ

Philippians 2:21(TEV)

Jesus is calling you into His service when He says, 'Seek first the kingdom of God and His righteousness and all these things shall be added to you.' With this statement Jesus reveals a fundamental characteristic of being in His service, and that is that you trust God to meet all your needs. Jesus said, 'Your Father knows what you need before you ask Him.' He said, 'Look at the birds of the air, for they neither sow nor reap nor gather into barns; yet Your Heavenly Father feeds them. Are you not of more value than they?' (Matthew 6:26-33).

Because you live in this world you must stay sober and vigilant not to become overburdened and consumed with the cares of this life instead of the cause of Christ. When the Apostle Paul was warned about the challenges he faced in serving Jesus he said, 'But none of these things move me; nor do I count my life dear to myself, so that I may finish my race with joy, and the ministry which I received from the Lord Jesus, to testify to the gospel of the grace of God' (Acts 20:24).

When sending His servants into the world to preach the Gospel, Jesus said that people's hearts are like the ground on which a farmer sows his seed. He warned that sometimes, because people's hearts are so hard, Satan will hinder what you say from having any effect and you will see no fruit. But don't let that discourage you, for there are others who will respond to the Gospel with joy and will join you in the church. Teach them the words I have given you so they will develop deep roots of faith in Me and can stand up when temptation comes and learn to follow Me in the Life you now live.

For the Life you now live you live by faith in the Word of God which lives and abides forever. Your whole life is a living testimony to the Word of God. Your faith is strong for you know God has never failed to take care of you and show you His steadfast love. So now that you have been enriched with all the wonderful blessings of the Life Jesus has with the Father, you have His power to preach the Gospel. 'Therefore go,' says the Lord, 'for I am with you. Always pray for those who are hurting and minister forgiveness. At every opportunity lay your hands on the sick in My name and they will recover.'

The fruit of the Life you now live clearly shows the Word of God is active and powerfully at work in you.

You are a true servant of Jesus Christ and live for Him.

Let's pray: Heavenly Father, You are so good to me. You give me all I need! My life is in Your hands! I praise You because You're always with me. Father, I love living and giving the Life Jesus has with You. I love serving You.

In Jesus' name, Amen.

And my God shall supply all your need according to His riches in glory by Christ Jesus

Philippians 4:19

It is beautiful to see what the grace of God had accomplished in the Church of Philippi. The Apostle Paul knew how severely they had been tested and how poor they were, so he encouraged them with the truth that the joy they were expressing through their extremely generous giving was none other than the grace of God.

You see these people had not just given what they could, but they kept giving and even pleaded for the privilege to serve God in this way. This grace of generosity was none other than the bountiful love of Jesus in them.

'Now you also are becoming progressively acquainted with and recognising more strongly and clearly the grace of our Lord Jesus Christ (His kindness, His gracious generosity, His undeserved favour and spiritual blessing), in that though He was so very rich, yet for your sakes He became so very poor, in order that by His poverty you might become enriched and abundantly supplied' (2 Corinthians 8:9 AMPB).

This grace of generosity is what lies at the very root of God's nature, for He is good and His mercy endures forever. There is no variation or shadow of turning in the light of God's loving-kindness, His goodness never diminishes and it is simply impossible for you to exhaust the riches of the glory of His goodness and grace.

Dear child of God, it is the Father's great joy to shower you with the richness of His grace and meet all your needs, for how well He understands what is best for you at all times.

Think about all the wonderful gifts of His grace that you have received now that you belong to Jesus. You are saved through the washing of regeneration and renewing of the Holy Spirit. You are justified by His grace and have become heirs of the Life Jesus has with the Father. And out of the fullness of this Life with the Father you are now abundantly supplied with one grace after another. And as if this generosity of His grace is not enough, it is only but the beginning of all the good things He has stored up for you.

So take off all the limits and let God enable you to be a generous giver, for Jesus said, 'It is more blessed to give than receive' (Acts 20:35).

Let's pray: Heavenly Father, Your grace so amazes me that You would enable me to be a generous giver. Help me to take off all the limits for I believe it is more blessed to give than receive.

In Jesus' Name, Amen.

But by the grace of God I am what I am, and His grace toward me was not in vain; but I laboured more abundantly than them all, yet not I, but the grace of God which was with me
1 Corinthians 15:10

Jesus, full of grace and truth, was able to do the works of God and the works He did testified that the Father had sent Him. Now, because Jesus is with the Father, you are enabled to do the works He does so the Father may receive glory through what Jesus works through you.

Jesus said, 'If you abide in Me and My word abides in you, you will bear much fruit.' The key to you being prosperous in the work of God is your personal relationship with Jesus. Are you daily living out of the fullness of the Life He has with the Father? Do you draw your strength from your union with Him? Jesus said, 'He who feeds on Me will live because of Me for without Me, you can do nothing' (John 6:57; 15:5).

Now it takes time to learn how to work by the grace Jesus supplies. His grace will enable you with superhuman strength to do His work. And while this is exhilarating, you have to learn how to stay calm and submitted to His Word and Spirit. You also have to learn how to rest and enjoy living every day to the glory of God.

Whenever we neglect to grow in grace we risk misrepresenting Him. The Scripture says that all we say or do should represent Jesus and glorify the Father (Colossians 3:17). We cannot therefore do without His grace.

The grace of Jesus will always produce in you an eager desire that in nothing you will be ashamed but that in all you are, say and do, Jesus will be magnified (Philippians 1:19-20)!

Jesus, the great teacher of grace and truth, will teach you through His Spirit to develop the discipline of staying one with Him to do the work of God and complete the task He has given you in such a way that glorifies Him.

Let us, like the Lord Jesus, glorify the Father on earth, by finishing the work He has given us (John 17:4).

Dear child of God, the all-sufficient grace of Jesus will renew your joy and strength in His service to labour more abundantly. Don't let anything deter you from finishing what He has given you - the pleasure and privilege to do in His service!

Let's pray, Heavenly Father, all I can do is sing Your praises for the glory of the grace You give me anew every day, so that in all I say and do, You are glorified.

In Jesus' Name, Amen.

Joseph is a fruitful bough, a fruitful bough by a well; his branches run over the wall. The archers have bitterly grieved him, shot at him and hated him. But his bow remained in strength, and the arms of his hands were made strong by the hands of the Mighty God of Jacob

Genesis 49:22-24

In the Bible, we see those who by the grace of God were given places of influence in the world to govern nations. Joseph, the young son of Jacob, stands out as an example as he learned to live by the grace of God in ways that inspire us all.

While Joseph was born with an incredible inheritance from his parent's obedience to God, his journey in life was fraught with difficulty, especially in his relationship with his brothers who hated him and eventually sold him into slavery. No matter what life threw at him, Joseph grew in grace and triumph in it all. Though he was tempted and wounded, his roots of faith grew strong in God, for the Lord was with him and - unbeknown to him - was working out His plan to give him a place by His grace to rule the world and bring about salvation for many, especially his own family.

The Bible shows that all of us, like Joseph, face temptation but that no temptation has overtaken us except such as is common to man. God who is faithful will not allow you to be tempted beyond what you are able to bear, for He will show you the way through (1 Corinthians 10:13). God says that you are blessed, happy and to be envied when you are able to be patient in your trials and stand up under temptation, for when you have stood the test and been approved, you will receive the victor's crown of Life, which He has promised to all those who love Him (James 1:12). This means that God, who is the source of all grace, will enable you to live a blessed life by making you complete, perfect, and lacking in nothing. He Himself will strengthen you, and like He did for Joseph, give you the place He has prepared for you in His service.

Over and over again, God shows through history how He desires to bless the world through those who are faithful to Him and long to see Him glorified. For Joseph this meant that he loved God no matter what. He learned from Him to forgive his brothers and he let God bless him in whatever he was going through. Joseph learned, while he was given great power and responsibility, to discipline his passions and not take what belonged to another. He learned to wait for God to give him what He had prepared for him, while living ready everyday by working hard and showing kindness to others.

Let's learn from Joseph how to appropriate the grace of God and live blessed by Him.

I pray God's grace makes you fruitful in the place He has given you in His service!

Let's pray: Heavenly Father there is nothing You cannot do and no purpose can be withheld from You. Here I am in Your service, living blessed by You. Thank You for making me fruitful in the place You have given me in Your service.

In Jesus Name, Amen!

In the same way you younger men must submit yourselves to the older men. And all of you must put on the apron of humility, to serve one another; for the Scripture says, 'God resists the proud, but shows favour to the humble.' Humble yourselves, then, under God's mighty hand, so that He will lift you up in His own good time

1 Peter 5:5-6 (TEV)

When I was young and struggling with submission, my father gave me some life-saving advice when he said, 'When you submit to those God has placed over you, you are submitting to God.' I have found this lesson to be essential in learning the meekness and humility found in Jesus. Truly, submission is the higher law! Especially when you begin to enjoy the blessings and power of the kingdom of heaven, you need to regularly visit the school of submission to maintain the humble, meek, sweet Spirit of Jesus.

You see, we can all suffer with discontent and struggle with the powers and influences that surround us. When we do, it is a strong indication that we need to find rest for our soul in our fellowship with Jesus. Jesus was pressed by every kind of power but remained totally at rest as He lived in the knowledge of the Father. He never felt threatened but maintained a sweet spirit. Nothing seemed too much for Him; He rose above every storm because He never lost sight of the Father in Him - in whom He had rest.

Come, dear child of God, you know that struggling and striving will never work what is right in God's sight. Don't be selfish and only think about your own affairs, but be interested in others too. When you feel angry, do not sin by letting the darkness in, for that would give the devil the opportunity to get a grip on you by twisting your thoughts with hate.

Don't let your mouth ever speak an unwholesome or unkind word, for this would grieve the Holy Spirit and sadden Him. Never hold a grudge and give way to bitterness, spite, ill will, indignation, rage or a bad temper. Resentment, quarrelling, slander or abusive- foul language – such things do not befit you! Jesus has given you a new tender heart filled with His love and compassion. He has made you ready and always willing to forgive others even as the Father has forgiven you. All this you receive in the school of submission, when you learn from Jesus to live in vital union with the Father, no matter what the condition of your life, relationships or work.

Oh, the joy of being clothed with a gentle, kind and gracious humble spirit so that, like Jesus, you may shine forth with the Father's love.

Let's pray: Heavenly Father, I humble myself and submit to You. Refresh, renew and restore my soul and give me rest in You so that in a gentle spirit I may serve those around me.

In Jesus Name, Amen!

Say to the righteous that it shall be well with them, for they shall eat the fruit of their doings

Isaiah 3:10

It shall be well with you! Jesus is the example of this, who committed no sin, nor was deceit found in His mouth; who when He was reviled, did not revile in return; and when He suffered and justice was denied Him, He did not threaten but rather committed Himself to Him who judges righteously. When Jesus died, His tender heart filled with love cried out, 'Father, into Your hands I commit My spirit.'

Now you know the end intended by the Lord, how Jesus is crowned with glory and reigns in majesty at the Father's right hand. Smith Wigglesworth once said, 'Don't ever waste a great trial for this is your robbing time, this is you coming into your inheritance.' You see, God is not unjust to forget the love you show for Him; He is a rewarder of those who diligently seek Him. The Scriptures leave no question concerning God's providence, they are filled with all the evidence you need to have hope through faith in God that it shall be well with you. As King David said, 'What would have become of me had I not believed that I would see the Lord's goodness in my life? In my discouragement I thought, 'They are lying when they say I will recover.' But what can I give to the Lord for all His goodness to me?' (Psalm 27; 116 LB).

Consider Job; God said that 'there is none like him; he is blameless and upright, he fears Me and shuns evil.' While Satan raged against Job and made him suffer because he was convinced Job would curse God and die, Job said, 'I know that my Redeemer lives, I know that in my flesh I shall see God whom I shall see for myself and my eyes shall behold Him, how my heart yearns in me!

For as long as I live, while I have breath from God, my lips shall speak no evil. I will not let my own heart reproach me for my conscience is clear' (Job 1, 19 and 27). The end of all Job's trials is not dissimilar to Jesus who prayed for our forgiveness. Job, who desired to see the Lord, said, 'I have heard of You by the hearing of the ear, but now my eye sees You, therefore I abhor myself and repent in dust and ashes.' At this point, God lifted Job's face in His presence and gave him the honour of praying for his friend's forgiveness. When he did this, God restored Job and gave him more than ever before.

Let this encourage you to look to God, be radiant with expectation and always be kind and forgiving, for it shall be well with you. Dear child of God, trust in the Lord, only believe, do not despair, be brave and of good courage, let your heart be enduring, for it shall be well with you! Remember, many are the afflictions of the righteous, but the Lord delivers him out of them all (Psalm 34:19).

Let's pray: Heavenly Father, I trust in You. I know You love me. I know You are with me. I know all shall be well.

In Jesus' name, Amen.

Bless those who persecute you; bless and do not curse

Romans 12:14

Remember, Jesus came to deliver you from the curse and bring you into the abundance of the blessings of the Father. Jesus did not come to condemn the world, but He came so that the world through Him might be saved. He taught that, like Him, we should bless and not curse, that we should bless even those who curse us (Luke 7:28).

Now it can be unbearably painful to suffer the cruel and unkind thoughts, feelings and words of those who curse you, especially when you love them and have done so much to bless them.

King David showed that he knew exactly what this feels like when he said, 'For it is not an enemy who reproaches me, for then I could bear it. But it was you, a man my equal, my companion and my acquaintance. We took sweet counsel and walked to the house of God together.' 'Help me, O Lord my God! Save me because You are loving and kind. Do it publicly, so all will see that You Yourself have done it. Then let them curse me if they like - I won't mind that if You are blessing me!' (Psalms 55 and 109).

You see when you are living in God's blessing, He turns all things for your good.

Jesus said to not let it bother you when you are reviled and persecuted and when people say all kinds of evil against you falsely. He said, 'When you suffer these things you should rejoice and be exceedingly glad, for great is your reward in heaven, for so they persecuted the prophets who were before you.'

Jeremiah, who was called the weeping prophet because of all he encountered in his service for God, said, 'Lord, You know it is for

Your sake that I am suffering. They are persecuting me because I have proclaimed Your word to them. Your words are what sustain me; they are food to my hungry soul. They bring joy to my sorrowful heart and delight me. How proud I am to bear Your name, O Lord. Yet You have failed in my time of need! Will they never stop hurting me? Your help is as uncertain as a seasonal mountain brook - sometimes a flood, sometimes as dry as a bone.' Then the Lord replied, 'Stop this foolishness and talk some sense! Only if you return to trusting Me will I let you continue as My spokesman. You are to influence them, not let them influence you! They will fight against you like a besieging army against a city wall. But they will not conquer you for I am with you to protect and deliver you, says the Lord' (Jeremiah 15:15-20 LB).

We need to remember not to take things to heart and dwell on what comes against us. If God is for us, who can be against us? This is what Jesus showed through His Life with the Father - He conquered every curse.

Dear child of God, do not let your heart be troubled. Rejoice in the Lord Jesus and again I say rejoice! He is your strength and song; He beautifies you with His blessings. So let all your thoughts be sweet and your words be kind. Your mouth is a well of Life, love and blessings and your tongue an instrument of healing.

You are blessed to be a blessing!

Let's pray: Heavenly Father, thank You for enabling me to bless and not curse and to speak words that impart grace and healing.
                                    In Jesus' Name, Amen.